WOODTURNING
with RESIN

Techniques & Projects
for Turning Works of Art

KEITH LACKNER

CEDAR LANE PRESS

Publisher: Paul McGahren
Editorial Director: Kerri Grzybicki
Design & Layout: Jodie Delohery
Illustrator: David Heim
Photographer (unless otherwise noted): Jacob Carr
Indexer: Jay Kreider

Cedar Lane Press
PO Box 5424
Lancaster, PA 17606-5424

Paperback ISBN: 978-1-950934-42-3
ePub ISBN: 978-1-950934-43-0

Library of Congress Control Number: 2021931063

Printed in the United States of America
10 9 8 7 6 5 4 3 2

Note: The following list contains names used in *Woodturning with Resin* that may be registered with the United States Copyright Office: Alumilite Corporation (Clear Slow); California Air Tools; Carter Products (Hollow Roller, Keith Lackner signature tool); Craftsman; General Finishes (Arm-R-Seal, Seal-A-Cell); Glass Vac; Global Wood Source; HUT Products (HUT Ultra Gloss Plastic Polish); Jacquard Products (Pearl Ex); JPW Industries (Powermatic); Marc Adams School of Woodworking; Micro-Surface Finishing Products, Inc. (Micro-Mesh); Mirka Ltd (Abranet); Stoner Molding Solutions; TMI Products (Stick Fast); TurnTex, LLC (Cactus Juice); *Woodcraft Magazine*; *Woodturning*; *WoodWorks* (David J. Marks); Yorkshire Grit; YouTube.

The information in this book is given in good faith; however, no warranty is given, nor are results guaranteed. Woodworking is inherently dangerous. Your safety is your responsibility. Neither Cedar Lane Press nor the author assume any responsibility for any injuries or accidents.

To learn more about Cedar Lane Press books, or to find a retailer near you, email Info@CedarLanePress.com or visit us at www.CedarLanePress.com.

DEDICATION

■ ■ ■ ■ ■

I would like to dedicate this to all the artists and craftsmen before me who have inspired and paved the way for me to carry on the traditions that have been passed down through the generations.

To David J. Marks: Thank you for being an inspiration to a whole generation of craftsmen and showing us that woodworking is more than just functional, but can be designed and built into beautiful pieces of art. Your work will always inspire me and my work, and your teachings are something I will always cherish, my friend. Thank you for everything you have taught me—it means the world to me. The classes I took at the David J. Marks School were instrumental in this book even being created.

To Mike Mahoney: Thank you for all the help you gave me early on and for guiding me into teaching. I will never forget you saying I would teach others someday. That one moment helped push me to be an instructor. I will always love the look in a student's eyes when they make something for the first time that I taught them; it is amazing to open the door for somebody else to pass into your trade, like you did for me.

To Carter Products: Lee Perez, you were the first one to see the potential in my early work and help nourish me by opening doors I would have never been able to open on my own. For that, I thank you. I also appreciate all of your hard work in bringing a turning product line to Carter Products. To Kris Scates, thanks for working with me to bring my signature tool to reality, and for always being there when I need help putting together the glass cabinet at the AAW shows. And finally, to Alex Snodgrass, my "big brother" in the woodworking industry. You have always been there to guide me and give me advice when I need it. I also really enjoy my luck at all the AAW shows getting to work side-by-side with a true craftsman and the master of the bandsaw.

To Mike, Don, and all the other great people who work at Alumilite: Thanks for making it possible for me to create the one-of-a-kind pieces I'm known for today. If it wasn't for your help and technical knowledge guiding me early on, I may have given up before I even really got started. A big thank you also to Alumilite for donating all of the resin used to create the projects in this book.

To JPW Industries (Jet, Powermatic, and Wilton): Thank you for making the absolute best woodworking equipment in the industry. Without your equipment, a lot of what I have done would not have been possible. Being in the Powermatic 2014 video will go down as one of the best accomplishments in my career. Many thanks also to Powermatic for donating the exhaust fan seen in the sanding photos.

To my wonderful girlfriend, Jessica: Thank you for understanding that late nights in the shop are something I need to do. Without your support at the shows and letting me work in the shop all day and night, none of this would have been possible. You allow me to be creative in my own special way.

FOREWORD

■ ■ ■ ■ ■

It isn't often that someone can break new ground in the field of woodworking and woodturning and gain acceptance for their work.

Keith Lackner is one of those individuals whose drive and passion pushed him to the forefront of what can now be referred to as a new category of woodturning: "hybrid woodturning." I see this term as a way to describe the combination of resin and wood. Keith wasn't the first one to do this, but he is the first one to take it to such a high level.

In one of my Creative Woodturning Classes back in 2013, Keith displayed the enthusiasm that I knew would take his work far beyond the others. Two years later, Keith returned to my school in Santa Rosa, CA, for a second class taught by guest instructor and world-renowned turner, Mike Mahoney. It was evident that Keith's sense of form had greatly developed since his first visit.

His fine eye for form, combined with the refinement of his techniques, moved him up the ladder quickly. While Keith always adhered to good, clean craftsmanship—the hallmark of quality woodturning—it was when he began experimenting with resin and playing with colors that his woodturning career started to take off.

I have always admired traditional woodturning and the rich beauty of nearly flawless natural wood. Bowls, hollow vessels, and boxes still grab my eye when they are carefully proportioned and finely detailed. However, perfect wood isn't always easy to come by, and if you like to turn highly figured woods and burls as Keith does, you are very likely to encounter defects such as bark inclusions and voids. Rather than view these flaws as problems, Keith started on his unique path by filling the voids with colored resin. He then somehow found a way to modify the curing equipment used for his smaller turnings to create larger-scale vessels and boxes with these resin techniques.

Today, almost a decade since his first class, Keith's creative and artful use of layered colors is what truly distinguishes him from the crowd. The recognition he garners for the beautiful, well-crafted, and unique vessels he creates at the lathe is rightfully earned.

David J. Marks
Designer/Craftsman
DJMarks.com

CONTENTS

■ ■ ■ ■ ■

PROJECTS

■ ■ ■ ■ ■

KIT HANDLES
60

PEN
70

DECORATIVE ART
76

BOWL
84

RIVER PLATTER
92

PINE CONE BOX
104

HOLLOW VASE
118

INTRODUCTION

■ ■ ■ ■ ■

My whole life I have been a creative person; whether drawing, throwing pottery, building and designing my own furniture, or woodturning, I've found ways to express my personality. I have always loved working with my hands and trying to create things. For the most part, I have gravitated toward working with wood; no two trees are the same, and I've always admired the beauty of the different tones and grain patterns of the seemingly endless species available. When I began working with resin, I noticed how perfectly the resin complemented highly figured woods with lots of imperfections and voids—wood that turners would usually pass on. At the time, no one was creating anything larger than a pen blank with these methods, but I could imagine the possibilities and wanted to push the boundaries to see what could be created.

THE BEGINNING

I started out, like everybody else at the time, by taking woodworking shop classes in high school. In one of my classes I made a coffee table with birdseye maple as an accent. Being introduced to

I created this larfe piece, *Grasshopper*, after being inspired by a creation made by my turning teacher, David J. Marks.

the unique and colorful patterns of highly figured woods helped to merge my love for woodworking with my love for art.

After graduating from high school, I made the decision to build all my own furniture—I wanted something that nobody else had, that would astonish people when they saw it for the first time. I was researching furniture makers, trying to find pieces that would leave me speechless. One night, I was flipping through the television channels and came across a show called *WoodWorks* with master craftsman David J. Marks. I remember being absolutely blown away by not only the design of the furniture but also the amazing wood he was using. I had no clue woods like that even existed. I became obsessed with watching *WoodWorks* every chance I could; I even built multiple pieces from the show. In a few episodes, David used the lathe to turn hollow forms—believe it or not, I had no interest in turning at that time.

Turning mixed wood
and resin pieces
is pretty similar to
turning just wood.

Teaching at
conferences and clubs
is one of my favorite
things to do.

TURNING ENTERS THE SCENE

A few years went by. One day, I made a trip to a
local tool supply store. A local turning club was
there allowing people to turn pens. I figured, why
not? I'll give it a try. In those 20 minutes, my life
changed—I became fascinated with woodturning.
In a few months, I got my first lathe. I found out
quickly that woodturning was not as easy as it was
in the store when I had somebody telling me how to
do everything. Back then, woodturning was not the
easiest thing to research, either. I pushed my lathe
into the corner and went back to furniture building.

A few months went by and I saw an ad from
David Marks selling olive wood. I thought it would
be so cool to own a piece of wood from somebody
I had followed and respected for years. I picked
up the phone and called the number from the ad.
I remember thinking that since David was a big
TV star, it must be a corporation I was calling. A
nice lady answered the phone; after I asked some

Mike Mahoney, seen here teaching me, was a huge influence in convincing me to become a turning teacher myself.

Taking a class with David Marks was a game-changer.

questions, she asked me to hold for David. I could not believe I was going to be talking to David J. Marks! He and I talked for what seemed like an hour, and at the end of the conversation, David invited me out to his school in Santa Rosa, California.

David's school is where I learned the art of turning. David showed me around his private wood collection, and I asked what his source was; I needed to go see all the exotic woods, and more importantly, burls. David directed me to Global Wood Source, just south of San Francisco. I walked in and was met by the owner, Russ Jacobs. When I told him I was at David's school, he gave me a full tour of his inventory. During this walk I noticed a pallet of highly figured walnut billets. Even though these billets had a lot of checks and splits, the grain was so insane I had to have them. I knew they were not safe to turn, but I figured with my woodworking experience I could veneer the pieces and use them as inlay in my furniture building. I had the billets shipped home to Illinois and put them up in my storage rack.

After having a taste of turning wood and resin, I knew it was something I wanted to keep doing.

THE FIRST PIECE

When I came home from David's school, I was obsessed with turning and did it day and night. It was getting close to Christmas, so I was making presents—lots of pens. One of the pen blanks I was turning was buckeye burl and resin. This was back in 2013 when these blanks were just released, and I remember thinking how unique they were. While putting the finishing touches on this pen at about 1:30 a.m., I thought how cool it would be if I could make a vase out of this material. Then, I remembered the walnut billets. They would be perfect—all the cracks, voids, and highly figured wood would blend in with the resin. Thus the idea for my first piece, *Hell Fire*, was born.

People often ask me how long it took me to make that first piece. I always smile and tell them one year. It wasn't just building a mold, pouring the resin, and *boom*—I had a blank. Absolutely nobody had cast anything of this size—15 times larger than a pen blank—so I had to invent every step of the way. Back then, the only blanks on the market were for pens or duck calls, and the only casting videos on YouTube (maybe a grand total of three) focused on making those blanks. All I knew was that the wood had to be dry and I needed a pressure pot.

After more research, I found the resin I needed was from the Alumilite Corporation. The next obstacle was to make a pressure pot that could handle a 14" x 20" blank and 80 psi. I think it took my friend Kyle and myself about 2 to 3 months to design and build a pressure pot that could build up the pressure in the time before the resin would set. The pour took 1 full gallon blend; since it's equal parts of resin and hardener, my very first cast was 2 total gallons.

While turning the large billet, I came across a crack running right down the center of the piece. I had nobody to turn to for advice, so I made the decision to recast the piece with black to replicate a black lightning bolt going right through the gold and red resin (see page 8). I showed this piece at AAW and got mixed reviews.

THEN WHAT HAPPENED?

I really needed to understand why my resin split, so I decided to call Alumilite's tech center. They were having a hard time understanding what I was talking about because I had used 15 times the amount they had ever heard of anyone using. They asked for me to send pictures, and about 35 minutes later, my phone rang. The owner of the company, Mike, told me they were blown away with what they saw and wanted to work with me. I agreed, as I knew I was on to something that no one had ever done before, and this was my chance to be the one who started it all.

And so, since 2013, I have continued to push the envelope with creating new techniques, and enjoy teaching clubs and people who want to cast large pieces so they do not struggle early on like I did. It is my hope that this book will answer your questions and put you confidently on the path to creating cool woodturned resin pieces!

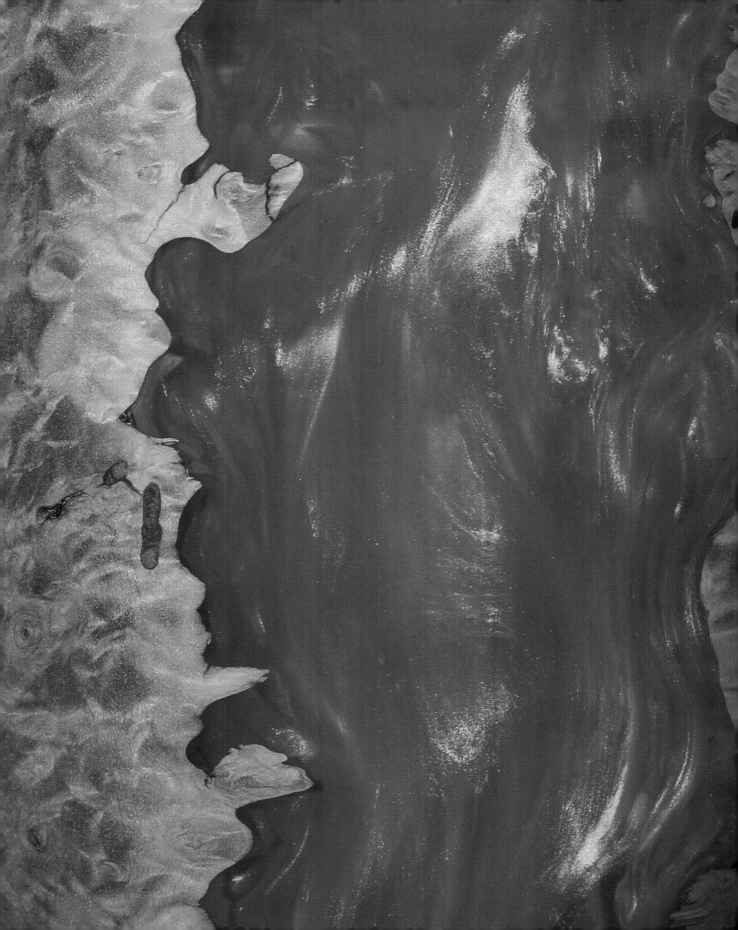

RESIN
AN OVERVIEW

■■■■■

This is where you'll start your informational journey into understanding resin. This basis in the theory of the overall resin-working process serves as an introduction to the unique properties of urethane resin. After reading this section, you'll have a firm grasp of what exactly resin is, what the different types are, and how to work with resin safely. You'll also understand the three golden rules of working with urethane resin—Preparation, Product, and Pressure. Mastery of these three areas will eliminate the majority of common issues encountered by resin hobbyists. Covered here is the importance of properly drying the wood used in a resin-fusion project; the what, when, and why of stabilizing woods; common mistakes to avoid when mixing resin; guidelines and timing for applying pressure to blanks; and much more.

WHAT IS RESIN?

The easiest way to explain resin is that two liquids are brought together (resin and a hardener, usually called Part A and Part B), and through a chemical reaction, the liquid turns into a solid mass that cannot return to the liquid form.

It is common for bubbles to form as the resin cures. An important part of working with resin is knowing how to remove those bubbles from your project before the resin hardens; the method depends on what type of resin you are using.

Urethane resin, the focus of this book, is fantastic for machining and yields a high gloss.

There are so many products and brands available in the world of resin that a beginner can quickly get overwhelmed. The three basic products that fall under the resin category are: polyester, urethane, and epoxy. A lot of times, people get confused on what product will work best for them, and some people do not realize that urethane, epoxy, and polyester are completely different products. Though we will focus on urethane resin in this book, it is useful to have a basic understanding of all three types.

Urethane

Urethane resin is the focus of this book. It is a liquid plastic that, when mixed with its hardener, cures into a hard but semi-rigid state; this quality makes it great for hobbyists and artists. It machines well; unlike epoxy, it can be buffed up to a glasslike finish or sanded down to matte. One of its cons is that it has a very short open time, and so it must be placed in a pressure pot to pulverize the bubbles before the resin sets. On the other hand, the resin cures significantly faster, allowing you to turn the piece in as soon as 48 hours after the resin has set. Readers should note that moisture coming into contact with uncured urethane will cause foaming and bubbling.

PROS

- Can be used for deep pours
- Machines the best of all the resins; can be buffed up to a high gloss (see photo above)
- Accepts colors well; the clarity allows you to show depth
- Short cure time allows quicker work time after casting
- Has UV prohibitors to stay clear longer
- Little to no odor
- Accepts finishes well

CONS

- Short open time
- Requires pressure to pulverize bubbles to a size the human eye cannot see
- Reacts negatively to moisture
- Some woods must be stabilized before casting

iStock.com/Malkovstock.

Epoxy is great for large projects, like this river table.

Epoxy

Epoxy is also a liquid that needs to be mixed with a hardener to activate it. It is a blend of polyamine and epoxide. Epoxy has a much longer open time than urethane resin, so a pressure pot is not required. Heat is applied to the surface to disturb the surface tension, allowing bubbles to float to the top and break up. Due to the longer open time, epoxy takes much longer to fully cure—up to one month. Another con is that it is extremely rigid when fully cured and can crack if it's placed over surfaces that expand and contract with the seasons.

PROS

- Long open time
- No pressure pot required
- Great for large projects like countertops and river tables (see photo above)
- Mix ratios are not that critical
- Moisture will not set off a chemical reaction

CONS

- A torch must be used to remove bubbles
- Longer open time means a much longer cure time
- After machining, cannot be brought back to a high shine; a thin top coat must be applied and cured perfectly
- Casting limited to between $\frac{1}{2}$" and 2" thick in one pour
- Over time UV exposure may cause yellowing

Polyester resin, applied in combination with fiberglass, makes a hard finish for boats.

iStock.com/Slavica

Polyester

Polyester is very hard and brittle, which does not make it a friendly product for woodturners or crafters. However, it excels in combination with fiberglass in the marine and automotive industry for reinforcement (see photo above). Polyester resin dries fairly rigid. A commonly known negative aspect of this product is the awful odor it gives off while curing. In fact, you should wear gloves and a chemical respirator when working with polyester resin.

PROS

- Very strong
- No pressure pot needed
- Can be applied to fiberglass to make a very strong material that can be used in many applications

CONS

- Very brittle
- If dropped it will shatter
- Prone to bad chip-out when machining
- Terrible odor

THE THREE GOLDEN RULES

Over the years and hundreds of casts, I have developed a set of rules that must be followed to have successful casts. I call these categories the three golden rules of casting: Preparation, Product, and Pressure.

Preparation: The Wood

Proper preparation of any wood you are going to have in your project is the first and most important part of casting with urethane resin. You'll need to clean the wood and make sure it is dry. In some cases, the wood will need to be stabilized; note there are plenty of types of wood that can skip that step.

Clean the wood. Select a piece of wood that has been stored in your shop for about a year. The first step in preparation is to make sure the wood is clean. It should be free from dust and dirt, and all bark should be removed from the wood. This is important—**you do not want anything to come between the resin and the wood.** This step will ensure a good bond. You will need these tools: a wire brush, dental picks, and a chisel.

Be sure the wood is completely clean. Use a wire brush, dental picks, and a chisel to remove all dirt and bark.

WHEN TO SKIP AHEAD

You can skip the Preparation rule—it focuses on prepping wood—and start with blanks made 100% from resin, like the kit handles starting on page 60. This way, if you are new to resin, you can get the feel for the process more quickly. Next, revisit the Preparation info to incorporate some wood that doesn't need stabilized (see list on p. 22). When you feel confident with that, go ahead and add stabilizing wood to your repertoire.

Remove moisture. Once the wood is completely clean and free of bark, it's now time for the most important step in casting with urethane—making sure to remove all moisture from your process. **Moisture and urethane resins do not get along and will cause a reaction**, whether you're casting with wood, plastics, or just resin.

When you purchase a piece of wood, there will always be moisture in it. There are two terms to describe how dry the wood is: "dry" and "green." Green wood has a high moisture content, usually 20% and above. Even industry-standard dry wood is considered too wet for casting (remember that any contact with water creates unsightly foaming, bubbling, and hazing in urethane resin), but it is closer. Most burls on the market are freshly cut, with a very high moisture content—sometimes as high as 30–40% moisture. These burls will need to sit until the moisture level gets down to about 17%. When I buy burls, I plan to use them next year. If you cannot wait that long, try to find a seller with burls that are not freshly cut. If you try to dry out burls with a high moisture content, the moisture will leave the wood at a rapid rate, causing internal checking in the wood. It will be hard to see the cracks until you begin to turn the wood, but this is a look you will not want in your finished piece.

The next step is to dry the wood out further by baking it. Since different woods lose moisture at different rates, it is impossible to tell exactly how long this process will take. It will take hours, and for some larger pieces, it could take days. Standard moisture meters do not read below 5%. When your meter does not respond in multiple spots and is cool enough to touch safely with your bare hands, the wood is now ready to be cast right away if it doesn't need to be stabilized.

We just spent all this time and energy removing moisture from the wood; if you are not going to cast or stabilize right away, it is important to wrap the wood in plastic wrap (vacuum-sealed bags are even better) until you are ready to go to the next step. Humidity in the air will absorb back into the wood; in a short time, the piece will be back up to 6–9% moisture, opening your project up to a failure.

Stabilizing: If Needed

This step is not always needed. It is technically part of the Preparation rule, but because it can sometimes be skipped, I've broken it out here for clarity.

First of all, what is stabilizing? Simply put, this is the process of using a vacuum chamber and vacuum pump to create the right conditions to completely saturate a soft piece of wood with stabilizing resin (note this is a different product than urethane resin). This resin is then activated with an external heat source (an oven), which stiffens the wood fibers, making them extremely rigid and hard. This process allows you to take a spalted, or punky, piece of wood and make it as hard and dense as an exotic species like ebony or a piece of Australian burl. You will need to stabilize any soft wood, including buckeye burl, maple burl, spalted woods, and pine cones.

Not always needed. Before we get too far into this aspect of working with resin, I want to state clearly that there are plenty of projects you can create that do not require the additional step of stabilizing wood. You simply create your blank either entirely out of resin, or use a wood that does not need to be stabilized. There are plenty of such woods to choose from: walnut, mesquite, cocobolo, Australian burls, and any very hard and dense wood. **You could create turned resin and fusion resin pieces for years and never need to bother with stabilizing.** In fact, I didn't start stabilizing woods until after working with resin for 3 years. However, once you are comfortable with resin turning and want to take it to the next level, you can broaden your choices even more by working with stabilized woods. You'll just need three new items: a vacuum chamber, a vacuum pump, and stabilizing resin.

Why stabilize? There are four main reasons for turners to stabilize. Punky woods have a unique look, but will tear out while turning if unstabilized. We all know about seasonal wood movement; by filling the spaces in the wood with hardened resin that humidity would normally get into, the wood is no longer affected by humidity and will not move. Stabilizing also seals the wood so it cannot be stained by any dye in the resin. For example, if you combine red-dyed resin with a light-blonde piece of maple burl, you will end up with maple that is pinkish in places—mainly the end grain. (If you'd rather not get into stabilizing yet, you can work around this problem by using only darker woods, or mica powders instead of dyes with lighter hard woods.) The final reason is balance. Resin weighs more than unstabilized wood; it can be very difficult to turn a blank with unbalanced, uncentered weight. Adding the stabilizing resin to the wood balances the blank.

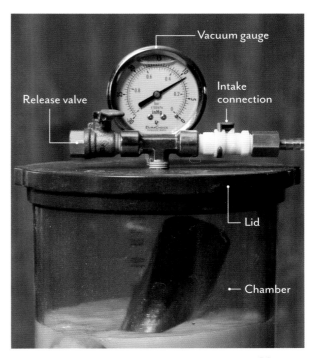

The vacuum chamber removes the air from the wood so the stabilizing resin can penetrate. Glass Vac (left) and TurnTex JuiceProof (right) are two commonly used vacuum chambers.

Necessary tools. There are several vacuum chambers on the market, including the Glass Vac and TurnTex JuiceProof. Get a two-stage rotary vane vacuum pump; they can reach a deep vacuum. The goal is to remove all the air from the chamber and the wood. Unlike the air compressor when pressurizing, the vacuum pump must remain on the entire time; don't worry about burning up your pump because running for long periods is what these pumps are designed to do.

Stabilizing at a glance. Here's a quick rundown of the stabilizing process. Place the wood in a vacuum chamber and completely submerge it in stabilizing resin (see photo above). A vacuum pump then removes the air from the chamber, and more importantly, the wood, creating the opportunity for resin to permeate. When the bubbling stops, that means all the air has been

sucked out of the wood and out of the chamber. Open the valve and shut off the vacuum pump, allowing air back into the chamber. (NOTE: If you turn off the pump without opening the valve first, the vacuum inside the chamber can pull oil out of the pump and contaminate the resin.) When the air is reintroduced into the vacuum chamber, it pushes down on the resin; the resin will absorb right away. This is why you will see the resin level drop very quickly when the valve first opens. To ensure deep penetration, the wood must soak in the resin.

Many people think that while under vacuum, the resin is being pulled into the wood, but this simply is not true. Think about submerging a dry sponge under water; very little water will absorb into the sponge because of all the air that is in its way. When you crush the sponge in your hand underwater (like creating the vacuum), the air is released. When you open your hand underwater

---

WHAT NEEDS TO BE STABILIZED?

Stabilize:

- All soft woods
- Pine cones
- Most burls, including buckeye, maple, and spalted woods

Don't Stabilize:

- Walnut
- Mesquite
- Cocobolo
- Australian burls
- Any extremely hard and dense wood

(like releasing the vacuum), the sponge can absorb all the liquid it can hold.

Now it is time to let the wood soak in the resin. It is difficult to say how long this process will take. I have left large pieces of buckeye in for days to make sure resin gets fully absorbed deep into the wood. Just remember, it's not possible to over-soak the wood.

The stabilizing resin then needs heat to set and become rigid, so the wood goes back into the oven. After any bleed-out is removed from the surface, the wood is ready for casting or storage. Once a piece is stabilized, there is no way for humidity to enter the wood. I've had pieces on the shelf for 6 months that went into a casting with no issues. One trick is to place the block in the oven for a few minutes before casting just to ensure there is no surface moisture on the wood.

Product: The Resin

Product—urethane resin, itself—is the second golden rule of working with resin. After you figure out how much resin you need to fill your mold (more on p. 38), the next step is to measure and mix the resin correctly. There are a few common mistakes at this stage.

Measure the correct amount. Many resins, including the product used throughout this book called Alumilite Clear Slow, have a 1:1 mix ratio by weight. This means that you need equal weights of Part A and Part B resin components. If you do not have the correct measurements, your piece can turn a hazy white color instead of clear, or there can be soft areas.

The easiest way to measure out the resin is to place a clear container on a scale, tare the scale, pour in Part A until you reach half the needed amount, and then top off with an equal amount of Part B (see photo on p. 23). NOTE: It doesn't matter which part you add to the other. Any scale will do, but I prefer a digital scale with a gram weight feature. When you measure by grams, the tolerances are very tight; this will ensure an accurate blend. If you are off a few grams due to a long pour or the scale not catching up in time, you can add a proportional amount of the other part so the extra first part is not wasted. However, with the size of projects we are working on in this book, being a few grams off does not affect the end product.

If you have a brand of resin that measures by volume, you will need a mixing cup that has volume measurements. The process is basically the same as by weight, but you won't need a scale. Simply pour each part to the correct line on the cup.

It's important to know that not all resins are measured by a 1:1 ratio. Some are measured by volume, others by weight.

Pour out the appropriate weight of each resin part.

Alumilite Clear Slow is my resin of choice for turning, and is measured 1:1 by weight.

Mix thoroughly. If you get lazy with the mixing process, your blanks will not cure properly. I prefer to mix my resin with a drill attachment in clear containers so I can see that it is properly mixed. Don't add color until you can see the base is combined. Use a scraper to make sure any material stuck to the sides and bottom get mixed in—they will not unless you take special care. Don't worry about mixing bubbles into the resin because the pressure pot will take care of them.

Add color. A great part of working with resin is the ability to add dyes to make your own custom blanks. It is very important to know whether the pigments are compatible with the resin. For example, urethane resins react violently with moisture, so do not use a water-based pigment. I find it best to use dyes sold by the manufacturer of the resin I use, as I know they will be compatible and there will not be any failures in the end product.

Mica powder allows intermingling of different hues without muddying the color.

Another option is mica powders, which reflect the light to give your blanks a whole new dimension. Because mica is made of individual small solid colored flakes, you can add batches of resin with different-colored mica powders to a mold to make a swirl of distinct colors (see photo above). This is difficult to do with dyes, as they will mix together into a brown color.

I recommend naming the color blends you come up with and keeping a recipe book of how much resin you mixed with what dyes so you can repeat the results.

Timing and temperature. There are a few important times to remember when working with urethane resin. **Open time** (also called work time and pot life) is the amount of time the mixed resin will remain in liquid form; a.k.a., how long it remains workable. This is how long you have from the second you combine the parts to get the resin under pressure so that the bubbles are removed before the piece cures. To provide a bit more detail: When you mix Parts A and B, you are kicking off the chemical reaction that ends in a cured blank. The chemical reaction is exothermic, meaning it creates heat as it cures. Open time is how long you have until the heat starts curing the piece; to be precise, manufacturers usually provide an exact temperature and sample mass with their open times. Alumilite Clear Slow has a 12-minute open time (100 g at 75° F), so I aim to get the mold in the pot in 10 minutes so the pot can pressurize in time.

If you can feel heat coming off your resin, the reaction has begun in earnest and the resin is starting to harden. I do not recommend pouring the resin into the mold after that because the pressure pot will not be able to pulverize all of the bubbles; your project will not have the nice, clear quality you want. You also do not want the ambient temperature or the temperature of the resin parts to be too high while working the resin, as that will shorten the open time even further. Most open times are calculated with ambient temperatures of 75° F. As you can imagine, the more resin you mix, the more heat is created. This means that larger batches have an even shorter open time. You can combat this by chilling the parts before mixing.

Demold time is how long it takes until the mixed resin is hardened enough to remove from the mold. Alumilite Clear Slow has a demold time of 4 hours, so I like to leave my pieces in the pressure pot for no less than 4 hours, but I've left pieces in the pot for as long as 2 days. For the most part, 4 to 6 hours is sufficient. I often cast right before the end of the day and let it sit in the pot overnight. This ensures a proper amount of time in

---

IMPORTANT TIMES FOR ALUMILITE CLEAR SLOW

- Open time: 12 minutes
- Demold time: 4 hours
- Cure time: 5 to 7 days

Pressure relief valve

Air outlet valve (optional)

Air inlet valve

Pressure gauge

Clamp

Lid

Body

A pressure pot is a must-have for working with urethane resin, but is pretty easy to understand.

the pressure pot. **Cure time** is the amount of time until the casting has completely hardened. Clear Slow has a cure time of 5 to 7 days.

The time period between demold and cure time is when you want to turn the piece. I usually recommend waiting until 1 or 2 days after demold time has passed.

Make sure that you read and understand the timing instructions of the particular resin that you are using.

Pressure: The Pot

Pressure is the third golden rule. Due to the short open time of urethane resin, a pressure pot must be used to create clear blanks. A pressure pot, in combination with an air compressor, uses air to push on the blank, compressing the air bubbles so they are too small to be seen by the human eye— then the resin cures under pressure so that the bubbles are never visible.

You can purchase a pressure pot (such as the 5-gallon model made by California Air Tools) or convert a painter's pot. Even though most paint sprayers operate at about 20 psi, the tanks are certified for much more. Especially if you want to cast larger pieces, you may have to convert a larger paint pot yourself. That being said, it is best to purchase a ready-made pressure pot unless you are experienced with the conversion process.

Get a compressor with a tank that is the same as or larger than the pressure pot. The air compressor tank can be smaller, but you will find that it will take longer to achieve the required psi due to the constant cycling to fill the pressure pot. You should also do a dry run first with an empty pressure pot to see how long it takes to achieve the desired psi in the pressure pot. The last thing you want is to have your casting fail because your pressure pot takes too long to get up to pressure.

Optimize pressure. Before I answer the question about how much pressure to use, let me explain best practices for optimizing pressure through correct mold construction. You want the air pressure to make contact with the resin and do what it needs to do. It is important to never stack anything on top of your mold, or you will be restricting that contact. This is also why I prefer to use horizontal molds—they give the air pressure more surface area to push down on the resin. A larger surface area will allow you to use less pressure.

For example: If you are casting a handle blank and you have a horizontal mold that is 6" x 1½" x 1½", that gives you 9 in.² of exposed surface that only needs to be pushed down 1½" to pulverize the bubbles. If you are doing the same blank as a vertical pour, it will be a little more difficult as you only have 2¼ in.² exposed, and the air pressure will need to compress 6" of resin. There is a greater chance of air bubbles in the vertical pour than the horizontal pour.

PRESSURE GUIDELINES

- **40 to 60 psi for smaller pours**
- **80 psi for everything else**

How much pressure? On smaller pours, 40 to 60 psi can be used, but on larger pours (anything over 2" thick), 80 psi is required to ensure there is enough pressure to pulverize all the bubbles. 80 psi is the sweet spot that will work for any project; however, not all pressure pots can handle that level of pressure, and it is very important to NEVER exceed the working pressures of your pressure pot. All pressure pots are not created equal and have different ratings.

A WORD ABOUT PRESSURE POTS

As mentioned, if you have a painter's spray pot, it can be converted to a resin pressure pot. There are plenty of videos available online if you are interested or curious about the process. However, make sure you fully understand and are comfortable with the conversion process. If you are uncertain at all, you should definitely purchase a ready-made pressure pot. There are several companies to choose from. Read all the instructions—and any other material you can find—until you understand the ins and outs of working with pressure pots. That said, don't be intimidated—plenty of people work safely with them every day. Your pressure pot is key to making beautifully clear resin blanks. You just need to follow your pot's guidelines, and never exceed the pot's pressure rating.

SAFETY

Though you may be up-to-speed on the safety issues around lathes, you probably aren't aware of the precautions required with resin and pressure pots. Take a look at these safety recommendations and be sure to follow them.

- Before using resin, always reference any safety data sheets. Do not use a product if you are allergic to it.

- Read and understand all instructions that are on the product you are using, as all resins are not the same.

- Always wear all the proper personal protective equipment. This includes a face shield, safety glasses, and a good mask when turning, and rubber gloves, safety glasses, and a mask if needed when casting the resin.

- Make sure to work in a well-ventilated area; use a good dust extraction system when turning and working with resin. If you have a small workspace or if you're not sure whether it is well ventilated, follow precautions for resins and use an appropriate organic respirator for safety.

- Always ensure that the gasket on the lid of your pressure pot is in place and free of any dirt. Also check the top of the pot for dirt or anything that could interfere with the tight seal between the pot and lid.

- Never exceed the recommended working pressures of your pressure pot. Not all pots are created equal and it is extremely important to know and understand what your pressure pot is capable of handling.

- Woodturning can be very dangerous if not done correctly. Make sure to read and understand all the safety procedures when using your lathe.

- Be sure that your workpiece is properly secured before starting your lathe.

- Tenons should be 40% of the total width of the project. For example, a 6"-diameter piece should have no smaller than a 2½" tenon. Additionally, the jaws of the chunk shouldn't be open more than ⅛" when fully closed around the tenon. Over half the length of the tenon should be in the jaws, but be sure not to bottom out. This is to ensure the wood face contacts the jaw face.

- Always start up your lathe at the slowest speed; gradually increase the speed. Your lathe should never shake or rock.

- Make sure to remove all rings and jewelry; if you have long hair, put it up in a pony tail.

- Use sharp tools. Remember: there is nothing more dangerous in a shop than a dull tool.

THE
PROCESS

· · · · ·

This section takes you into the nitty-gritty, step-by-step processes of working with resin. We'll start with an overview of the tools you'll need. The overall process begins when you prepare the wood you're going to be joining with resin (unless you choose to make 100% resin pieces). Create the mold that will form your blank, then properly mix the resin and add it to the mold. After allowing the resin to set in the pressure pot, mount the blank on your lathe and turn it. Finally, we'll go through the finishing process for both resin and resin-fusion pieces and cover some common troubleshooting issues. After absorbing this section, you'll be ready to start turning projects.

TOOLS YOU'LL NEED FOR RESIN

In an effort to keep the step-by-step projects' tools and materials lists shorter, you'll find an inventory here to help you keep track of what special tools you need for working with resin. Experienced turners will already have most of the required equipment except for these items. More detail about tools will be given throughout the book as they are used. A more detailed list of everything you'll need to make the projects is in Resources.

Gather the tools and materials you'll need to work with resin.

RESIN TOOL KIT

- Rubber gloves, glasses, and mask
- Moisture meter
- Wirebrushes
- Wood chisel
- Dental picks
- Vacuum chamber
- Vacuum pump
- Stabilizing resin
- Oven with tray
- Rice

- Scale with gram measurements
- Clear plastic containers with volume marks
- Stopwatch
- Drill and mixing attachment
- Scraper
- Reusable molds
- Thin stick for colored resin manipulation

- Urethane mold release spray, such as Stoner
- Pressure pot
- Air compressor
- Replaceable carbide-tip round-nose tool, such as Keith Lackner signature tool
- Water-sanding pads, such as Micro-Mesh, in 2,400, 3,200,

4,000, 6,000, 8,000, 12,000, 15,000, and 20,000 grits
- Plastic polish, such as HUT Ultra Gloss Plastic Polish, and soft cloth
- Friction polish, such as Yorkshire Grit
- Jeweler's polish and buffing wheel

PREPARING THE WOOD

Preparation of any wood to be included in the blank is the first golden rule of working with resin, though remember you can skip this section if you plan to start with 100% resin pieces. Here is how to make sure that the wood you use is ready to include in a mold. After you select a piece of wood from your collection that is below 17% moisture, you'll clean it thoroughly and dry it further.

1. Clean the wood. Select a piece of wood that has been stored in your shop for about a year. Thoroughly clean the wood by scrubbing it with a wire brush to remove dirt. If needed, use a wire brush attachment on your drill. Don't be afraid to try different sizes and bristle types until you find a combination of tools you like.

2. Remove bark. Any bark should be removed with a chisel. Dental picks can also be useful for getting into tight crevices in the wood. Bark tends to loosen and detach from the wood. If left on, the resin will attach to the bark and not the wood itself. Over time, the bark will detach from the wood, allowing the resin to fall off with the bark.

3. Check moisture level. Measure the piece's starting moisture level. If it is not 17% or below, allow it to air-dry until it is. if this happens, select an older piece that is more likely to be at the correct percentage.

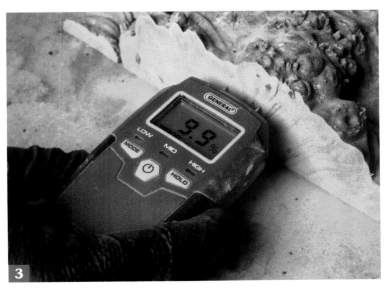

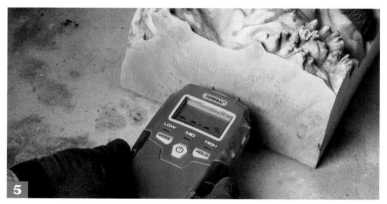

4. Bake the wood. Preheat an oven to 220° F. Water boils at 212° F, so the oven needs to be set higher than that. Place the wood in the oven.

5. Confirm lack of moisture. Check moisture level periodically. When the piece has no measurable moisture, you're ready to proceed. This could be hours or days depending on the piece. If you're not going to move on to casting or stabilizing the piece immediately, wrap it with plastic wrap or vacuum-seal it to prevent moisture from being reintroduced.

STABILIZING THE PREPARED WOOD

Remember, not all wood needs to be stabilized (see p. 22). But if you do, here are the steps to follow.

In order to know what level to run the vacuum pump to, you need to know your altitude relative to sea level. After that, search online for a maximum theoretical vacuum calculator. I recommend visiting TurnTex's help center online.

1. Set up the vacuum chamber. Put the dried and cooled wood (you should be able to safely pick it up with your bare hands) in the vacuum chamber and add stabilizing resin (such as Cactus Juice) until there is at least ½" of stabilizing resin above the wood; place a weight on top to keep it from floating up. Close up the pot.

2. Begin vacuuming. Turn on the vacuum to remove the oxygen from the pot. You will see the chamber begin to foam up. This is the air that is deep in the fibers being extracted—you are removing it from the wood so the resin will then be able to have a path into the fibers.

3. Regulate the valve. You should open and close the valve during the initial vacuuming so the resin doesn't get sucked up into the pump. The pump must run the whole time during the process. Keep track of how long it takes for the bubbling to stop. Be sure to read the manufacturer's notes on the pump.

4. When the foaming stops, you're done. Open the valve and turn off the pump, allowing air back into the chamber. This allows the resin to soak in. Though time to complete the process varies based on the piece, if you allow a bit longer than it took the bubbling to finish, that usually does the trick. One great thing is you can't leave it in too long because once it's full, the wood will just stop absorbing.

5. Into the oven. Place the wood on an aluminum tray and into an oven or toaster oven (not one used for cooking) preheated to 220° F. Bake for at least as long as it took to absorb the resin. The stabilizing resin can't over-activate, but it can be under-activated, so it's always best to bake a bit longer. After the wood has cooled, use a grinder, sander, or mini motorized cutting tool to remove any bleed-out on the surface. Now the wood is ready for casting or storage.

MAKING A THROWAWAY MOLD

Molds are simply a watertight chamber used to hold the resin for casting. Molds can be made from many different materials and break down into two types: throwaway and reusable (see photo on p. 37).

Throwaway molds are great for larger pieces or projects with odd dimensions. I like to use medium density fiberboard (MDF) for squared-off molds.

Make a Squared-Off Throwaway Mold

All you need to create a squared-off one-use mold is your cutting method of choice (I prefer a tablesaw), the piece of wood you want to fit in the mold (or a rough idea of mold dimensions), and some hot glue.

1. Measure and cut the bottom. To make an MDF mold, measure and cut the bottom piece first. As seen here, if you have a squared-off piece in mind, you can move a tablesaw blade so the piece fits between it and the fence. You now have the correct width for the bottom. Repeat with the other dimension.

2. Measure and cut two sides. Cut two sides to the same width as the base. Measure how high the sides need to be and transfer that measurement to the tablesaw. Cut the two sides to that height.

3. Measure and cut the remaining sides. With the saw off, place the base flat and stack the two sides next to it to get the length of the remaining two sides. Cut the two opposing sides to that width, and then cut to the mold height.

4. Glue the mold together. Use hot glue to secure all the sides. Hot glue also ensures a water-tight fit.

5. Apply extra sealing. Just for added measure, run a bead of hot glue around the joints of the interior and exterior of the mold.

Make a Round Throwaway Mold

If you want to make a project that is round and relatively flat, like the River Platter on page 92, it is most efficient to create a round throwaway mold.

1. Cut the tube. Using your cutting method of choice with appropriate safety equipment and jigs, slice off a section of concrete tubing form. I recommend a bandsaw with a jig and wedges to keep the tube from rolling. If you're including wood in the blank, use the tube to trace a curve onto the burl.

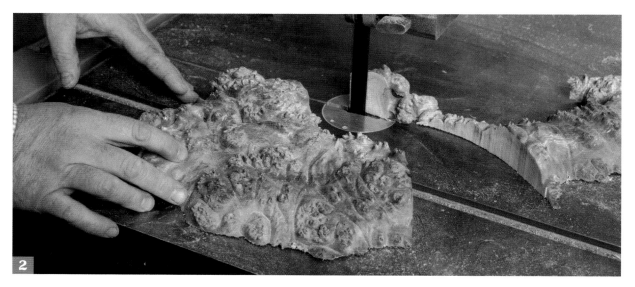

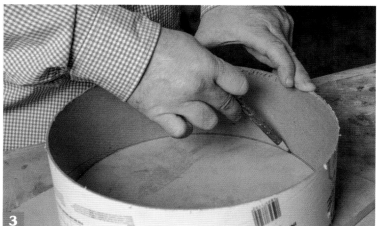

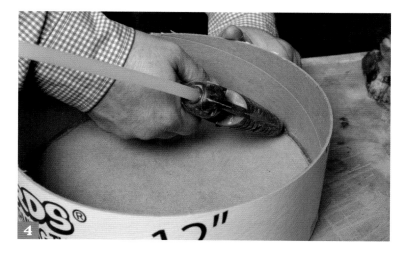

2. Cut the wood pieces. Cut out the burl pieces on the bandsaw.

3. Cut out the mold bottom. Place the tube on top of a piece of MDF and trace the interior circle of the tube. This will be the bottom of the mold. Cut it out on the bandsaw.

4. Attach the mold pieces. Use hot glue to attach the bottom inside the tube. Be sure to run a bead of glue around the inside and outside joints.

USING A REUSABLE MOLD

These molds are made out of material that allows the resin to release without damaging the mold. Common materials used are silicone, PVC, and ultra-high molecular weight (UHMW) plastic. These molds can be used over and over again and are highly recommended for casting pen blanks, tool handles, and jewelry pieces. For a great example, see the slab blank on page 63. You should use a reusable mold for any sizes that you cast repeatedly as it will save you time and money in the long run. Most reusable molds are assembled with panhead screws; the screws will pull the sides tight, ensuring a watertight seal. There are some molds that are one piece and do not have screws.

Pictured here are a variety of molds, both throwaway (the brown ones) and reusable (the others).

GETTING READY FOR RESIN

1. Attach the wood. After you've created or purchased your mold, the next step is to affix any wood you want in the blank to the mold. You can use hot glue for smaller pieces; place a bead of glue around the edge of the wood, back a bit from the edge. Don't be shy about adding glue to the center area.

2. Secure the wood, if needed. The wood is now affixed to the mold. Keep in mind that some reusable molds don't work well with hot glue. Also, large blanks often produce too much heat during the curing process, which can re-melt hot glue. In those cases, place a screw into a waste area of the wood to attach it to the mold.

3. Measure out the rice. Figure out how much resin you need to mix by measuring dry rice into your mold. Count how many cups (by volume) you add.

4. Level the rice. Pat down the rice so you can tell if it is at the right level. It isn't exact, but it will get you close enough.

5. Record the rice amount. Write down how many cups of rice you added.

6. Calculate your resin needs. If you're using Alumilite Clear Slow resin, refer to the conversion chart on page 136 to see how much resin you'll need. If you use a different brand of resin, you'll need to create your own conversion chart; see instructions for filling the blank chart on page 137. Write how much of each part of resin you'll need on the mold. Once you have completed the calculations for your particular resin, remove the rice.

7. Apply release spray. If you're using a reusable mold, apply mold release spray, making sure not to get any on wood surfaces that you want to bond with resin. You can also spray the mold before you add the wood, though you will then need to place a small screw through the mold near the top of the wood to create a stop so the wood does not float. Hot glue will not adhere after the mold has been sprayed.

MIXING THE RESIN

After your mold is ready to go, the next step is preparing the resin. It is very important to read the instructions of the product to ensure success. Before you start to mix the resin, you should know what the manufacturer has to say about open time, demold time, and mixture ratios, as well as any special advice regarding your particular product.

1. Measure the resin. The urethane resin I use, Alumilite Clear Slow, needs to be measured out as a 1:1 ratio by weight. I do this by pouring part A into the container, then taring the scale and pouring an equal weight of part B into the same container. Following the directions for your resin, measure out the parts you need. Remember— as soon as the two parts come into contact, start your stopwatch to mark open time.

2. Mix it together. Place the mixing attachment into the resin first and then turn on the drill. Don't worry about mixing bubbles into the resin; the pressure pot will get them. Make sure you stop periodically and scrape the sides to ensure a proper mix. There should be no visible swirls when you're done.

3. Mix in colors. If you want to have color in your piece, add dyes and mica powders into separate cups, then add your resin and thoroughly mix. Be sure to switch to a clean mixing attachment between colors or wipe off the attachment thoroughly. Remember, it is important to use a dye that is from the same manufacturer as your chosen resin. Document the different recipes you create so that you can reproduce your favorite results—it is useful to record how much dye or mica powder was mixed into how much resin, and what the overall percentage of total resin each color is within the project itself.

4. Add resins to the mold. A high-up pour will create a natural splash look; manipulation will cause tight swirls. If you gently move a thin stick with smooth, flowing strokes, you can create the illusion of movement in the resin without mixing it. Have fun experimenting with different ways of adding the resin colors to the mold and record your results. There is no need to tap or jiggle the filled mold—the pressure pot will take care of getting the resin nice and flat. You're now ready to apply pressure to the mold. Hopefully you have a few minutes left on your open time countdown.

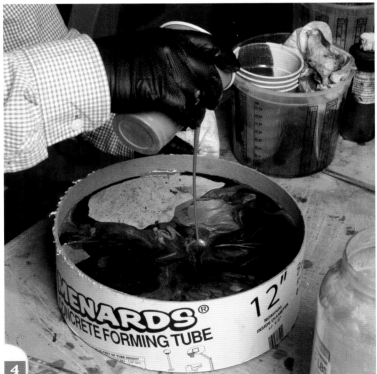

APPLYING PRESSURE

Now it's time to let the pressure pot do the work. This step of the process squeezes the bubbles in the resin, making them too small to see, and keeps them that way until the resin cures and freezes them in place.

1. Prepare the pressure pot. Check the sealing gasket and the top rim of the pressure pot for any dirt that will keep the lid from sealing. Gently place the filled mold into the pot. If you created a mold that isn't flat on the bottom, you can nestle it into some rice to keep everything level. Close the top, making sure to tighten each wingnut or clamp. I recommend tightening opposite pairs together.

2. Add pressure. Attach the air compressor and begin adding pressure to the pot. Most pots have a diverter welded to the air intake to keep the air from splashing the resin. If yours does not, be sure to add pressure slowly. NOTE: Follow the resin manufacturer's recommendations for psi and be sure not to exceed your pressure pot's safety limit. Once the pressure is correct, detach the air compressor.

3. Count down to demold time. Now, we wait. The mold should remain under pressure until the recommended demold time of your resin has been reached. There is no harm going past this time. When ready, you should slowly bleed the pressure out of the pot. You don't want to release all of the pressure at once, just in case. Open the lid and remove the solidified mold.

Allow the mold to sit for an additional 1 to 2 days to ensure it has fully cured.

4. Separate the blank. If you are using a reusable mold, you should be able to remove the blank by thumping it upside-down on a solid surface. If the mold was connected with screws, you can loosen those to aid blank removal. Sometimes a chisel can help to separate a stubborn blank from the mold. Throwaway molds require a bit more work. Unscrew any anchor screws and then apply your cutting method of choice to remove the walls of the mold, being sure to keep as close to the edge of the blank as you can.

5. Cut the blank, if needed. If you've created a slab blank that needs to be cut apart into different pieces, do so now using your cutting method of choice.

TURNING RESIN

Now, the exciting part: turning and shaping your creation. **Resin turns with the same fundamentals as traditional woodturning**, so I don't go into much detail here. Refer to your favorite turning manuals for information on the basics. I'll point out some helpful information for working with resin using the most common turning tools, as well as sharing my favorite tool and grind angle to use. There are also a few tricks that I have learned over the years. The most important thing when turning resin and mixed composition pieces (other than creating a shape you're pleased with, of course) is to **leave as smooth a surface with your cutting tools as you can**.

Replaceable Carbide-Tip Tools

One piece of advice I can offer is that resin really does like to be scraped. That is why I feel the carbide-tipped cutter is the most efficient tool to use through most of turning with resin (see photo below). These recent arrivals to the turning scene received a bad rap at first because they were introduced as an all-in-one turning tool. But, like all turning tools, there is a time to use these and a time to leave them in your tool rack. Carbide-tipped tools are basically traditional scrapers, but they do not cut with a burr; they use a removable carbide tip that lasts many times longer. When the tool becomes dull, simply loosen the attaching screw, rotate the tip or replace it, and tighten the screw: you are back to turning with a fresh edge. The long wear time and lack of sharpening maintenance is why these tools excel in turning resin. To properly use a carbide-tip tool, put the cutting edge at the centerline and introduce the cutting edge into the blank.

Some of the carbide-tip tools on the market are a little too aggressive when it comes to cutting resin. This is why I created a design specifically for cutting resins and dense hardwoods (see photo at top right). The Keith Lackner signature tool from Carter Products has an acute angle of 30°, allowing smooth cuts without self feeding. It also has a smaller cutterhead for more efficient resin removal.

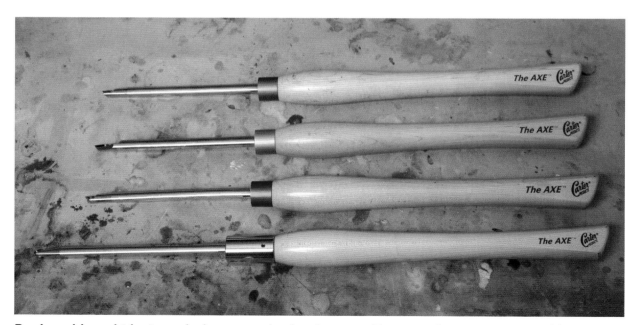

Replaceable carbide tip tools do not need to be sharpened because the tips are removable.

My 30°carbide-tip tool is great for turning resin, dense exotic woods, end grain, and hollowing out vessels.

Carbide-tip scrapers are the only kind of scraper you should use on resin projects.

Traditional Turning Tools

If you're looking to stick with turning tools you already own, there are a few options. Basically, almost any tool you use for turning wood can be used on resin and blanks made of wood and resin. Read on to find out what tools are best and which to avoid.

Scrapers. Scrapers use a burr to cut just below the centerline of the piece by scraping across the wood. One of the scraper's biggest downfalls is that its burr dulls more quickly than other tools, and fails even quicker with resin. Traditional scrapers work great with regular woodturning; however, resin destroys the burr almost the second it touches the workpiece, so I do not recommend using traditional scrapers on resin. Go with a replaceable carbide-tip tool instead.

Elliptical bowl gouge. The most universal of the gouges, the elliptical bowl gouge can be used for bowl and spindle turning, as well as turned so the flute is facing the workpiece and used as a sheer scraper. This is my favorite traditional turning tool for resin and resin-fusion (resin and wood) pieces;

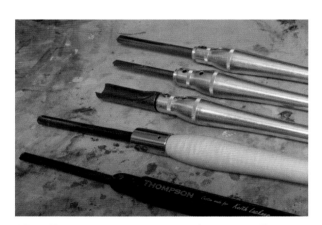

The elliptical bowl gouge works very well on resin pieces.

in my opinion, it is the best all-around tool for refining shapes and cutting in crisp details.

Spindle gouge. The spindle gouge is a traditional gouge used primarily in spindle turning. With its swept-back wings, it excels in small intricate work, and does fine with resin.

Spindle-roughing gouge. This gouge is primarily used for bulk removal in spindle turning. With its forward wings, it excels in bulk removal and getting shapes to the round very quickly. Unlike the

The spindle gouge is useful for detail work on resin pieces.

The ⁴⁰⁄₄₀ grind has a cutting-edge angle and wing sweep backs of 40°.

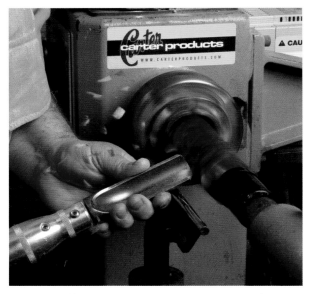

The spindle-roughing gouge is essential for rounding a blank mounted in spindle position.

other two gouges, the spindle-roughing gouge can only be used to turn wood that is oriented with the side grain exposed, like in spindle turning. There will be a catastrophic effect if attempting to cut edge-grain fibers. It works well on resin and resin-fusion pieces that are hollow forms, lidded boxes, pens, and handles.

Best grind. There are many grinds you can put on your gouge. In my opinion, the best grind to use is a ⁴⁰⁄₄₀ grind on an elliptical bowl gouge (see photo above). This means the angle of the cutting edge is 40° and the wings are swept back at 40° for better chip removal. The ⁴⁰⁄₄₀ is the only grind that excels in both soft woods, hard woods, and extremely dense exotic woods, in both push and pull cuts, leaving a sandable finish. This makes it great for resin turning, especially resin with wood in the same block.

High-speed steel. HSS stands for high-speed steel. Within the class of HSS, there are different blends of steel that far exceed the rest. Frankly speaking, you get what you pay for. The main difference is the amount of carbon in the steel—my favorites are M42 and V10. Some tool makers even give their tools cryogenic treatment, which enables the edges to hold a lot longer and sharper than most steel. Remember: just because a tool is HSS doesn't mean that it's the best steel to buy. Make sure you do your research and understand what steel you really are buying if you don't want to spend all day sharpening your tools instead of turning.

When you have the lathe speed and tool travel speed adjusted properly, you will see nice ribbons flying off your piece.

Speed

The biggest trick I discovered with turning resin is speed: both the RPMs of the lathe and the travel speed of your tool. Once the piece is rounded, I prefer the lathe at spindle-turning speed, which is roughly 2,000 RPMs. As far as the tool traveling across the workpiece, you should always maintain a slow and fluid cutting speed. If you find yourself pushing through the cut, producing powder, and starting to feel heat, you could be pushing too fast; this puts strain on the resin and can cause it to chip out. (Though, keep in mind that another cause of this phenomenon is a dull tool—you may just need a fresh edge.) If this happens, increase the RPMs or slow down your tool travel cutting speed. When done correctly, you should see a beautiful ribbon flying off your piece (see photo above).

If you are using the correct lathe and tool-travel speeds and are still having problems, sharpen your tool.

FINISHING RESIN

This part of the process will make your project shine. I find that finishing is an overlooked but extremely important part of our craft. When finished correctly, your piece should leave others in awe, especially when the light bounces off the resin.

Dry-Sanding

The first step in finishing is doing regular sanding up through the grits. Since your piece is on a lathe, the easiest way is to reduce your lathe RPMs by at least 20% from the speed at which you turned the piece, and get sanding.

What's actually going on when you sand? You're cutting into the material with a series of scratches, gradually making the scratches smaller and smaller, until you have a smooth surface. The lower the grit number, the more aggressive and deeper the scratches are. The most important thing to remember is to never jump grits too aggressively,

GRIT ORDER: DRY-SANDING

- 80
- 120
- 220
- 320
- 400
- 600   **STOP HERE** if applying a surface or penetrating finish.
- 800
- 1,000   **STOP HERE** if water-sanding.

especially in the beginning—if you do, you will never be able to remove the scratches left from the more assertive grits. Never jump more than 100 grit before you reach 400-grit level.

When it comes to sandpaper, I recommend Abranet. In my opinion, it is the best sandpaper on the market. It is designed to remove material and the perforated back keeps the paper from clogging like regular sandpaper will, especially in the early grits (see photo below). For the 1,000-grit sanding rounds, I prefer to use 0000 steel wool.

Another thing to keep in mind: most lathes are equipped with forward and reverse options. I highly recommend sanding each grit in both forward and reverse, especially in the lower grits. The grit you start with depends on how rough your surface is after turning but the worst-case scenario is 80 grit. Be sure to decide what your next finishing steps are so you can stop dry-sanding at the appropriate grit. See the box below for the grits I use in the order that I use them.

If we were turning wood, this is where I would stop and start to apply my finishes, but since we are turning resin, this is just a good base for us to bring it to the next level.

Abranet sandpaper excels at removing material without clogging.

Immerse the water-sanding pads in a container of water when you start dry-sanding so they are saturated when you need them.

Squeeze a wet towel above the workpiece as you water-sand.

Water-Sanding

Water-sanding is similar to dry-sanding, but with much finer grits. I prefer this for all-resin pieces, such as the kit handles shown later. Water-sanding is not a good choice for pieces with wood. The texture of wood, even when highly sanded, creates too much friction with the Micro-Mesh pads. The piece ends up pulling and grabbing the pads, which can even burn into the wood in the worst-case scenario.

The pads need to be saturated with water to avoid building up heat and melting into the resin. One trick I use is to submerge the pads in water

when I start finish turning (see photo above). This way, they will be well saturated by the time I need them. A second tip is to squeeze a wet towel directly above the workpiece as needed to keep clean water between the pad and the workpiece (see photo on p. 49). This step will also pick up any dirty water, taking away the chance to clog the pad.

I recommend Micro-Mesh pads for the water-sanding process. I start with 2,400 and work up to 20,000 grit. See the box on page 49 for the grits in the order that I use them.

The next step in water-sanding is to hit the piece with polish. Use a high-gloss polish specifically made for polishing plastic, such as HUT or Yorkshire Grit. With the lathe running, apply using a rag. Increase the speed 20% and burnish in. Apply enough pressure so the rag is feeling warm, but not hot.

Finally, add jeweler's polish to the buffing wheel and buff the resin to a high shine.

GRIT ORDER: WATER-SANDING

■ 2,400	■ 8,000
■ 3,200	■ 12,000
■ 4,000	■ 15,000
■ 6,000	■ 20,000

FINISH CHOICES

- **All resin:** Dry-sand 80 to 1,000 grit; water-sand 2,400 to 20,000; plastic polish; buff.

- **Resin/wood simple:** Dry-sand 80 to 1,000; buff.

- **Resin/wood intermediate:** Dry-sand 80 to 600; surface or penetrating wood finish; plastic polish; buff.

- **Resin/wood special:** Dry-sand 80 to 600; spray lacquer; dry-sand 800 to 1,000; resin parts only, water-sand 2,400 to 12,000.

- **Resin/wood for heavy use:** Dry-sand 80 to 600; wood only, penetrating oil; 3–5 layers wipe-on poly, sanding with 0000 between each layer.

Finishes for Resin-Fusion Pieces

These are my preferred finishing techniques when I have a piece with both wood and resin. After dry-sanding up to 600 grit, now is the time to make the wood pop by applying a wood finish (more detail on that in a bit). Next, polish the piece with HUT or Yorkshire Grit, and finish by buffing with jeweler's polish.

A more concise wood and resin project finish is to dry-sand to 1,000 grit and then buff with jeweler's polish. For the most part, finishes for woods fall under two categories: surface and penetrating finishes.

Surface-cured finishes. These are finishes that adhere to the surface and build up in layers, making for a strong finish—the type of durable finish you'd want on a piece you're going to touch and use often. You have the option to buff up to high gloss or leave the piece with a dull matte finish. When using surface-cured finishes, **it is important not to**

Surface-cured finishes, like polyurethane, are built up in layers.

With a buffing wheel, jeweler's polish, Yorkshire Grit, and water-sanding pads, you can make your resin shine.

Charge the buffing wheel with jeweler's polish so you can buff your project.

sand to a very high grit, as these finishes need the lines left behind from 600-grit paper to hold on to. Sanding to too high of a finish will make the surface very slick; you will struggle with runs in your finish. Finishes that fall into this group are: polyurethanes, lacquer, and shellac.

To apply a surface-cured finish, first clean the surface of any dust or particles. Apply the finish with thin, even strokes. I prefer using a clean cotton T-shirt that has been cut up and folded into squares approximately 3" x 3". Put the piece in a dust-free space that is above 70° F; colder spots will prolong the cure time. Wait a minimum of 24 hours. Sand lightly with 0000 steel wool. Blow off any dust and reapply finish. Repeat as many times as needed to achieve the finish you're happy with.

Another variation with stunning results for fusion pieces is to use gloss spray lacquer. With the piece off the lathe, lightly spray on a thin, even coat to the whole outside. Leave to dry in a dust-free area. Once dry, build coats with more spray. After three coats, I like to let it sit for a few days to

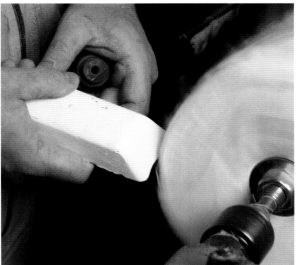

give the lacquer a good amount of time to harden. Sand the whole surface with 0000 steel wool and repeat the process so far. Now, do the inside and the bottom of the base as you did the outside. Make the wood parts a satin finish by finishing with 0000 steel wool. On the resin parts, after 0000

A woodburned signature is the finishing touch.

steel wool, water-sand up to 12,000 grit. This will take some time, but the finish will be worth it; the contrast between the warm satin glow of the wood and the glasslike reflection of the resin will set your pieces apart.

Penetrating finishes. These finishes penetrate deep into wood fibers and cure beneath the surface. They work great as a base finish when dealing with highly figured woods. This is called "popping the grain," due to the fact the oil penetrates deep into the fibers of the woods and really enhances the different tones of the wood. This process yields really stunning results with burls because of the combination of end and side grains, and usually the presence of some compression curl. Some examples of penetrating oil are: tung oil, boiled linseed oil, and mineral oil.

First, apply a penetrating oil to the wood only. I like to use General Finishes' Seal-A-Cell. Since resin does not have fibers, the oil will not penetrate

it. It won't hurt anything if you get some oil on the resin, but there is no need to make sure it is coated. Turn the lathe on about 20% faster than turning speed; move your hand as slowly as necessary to feel comfortable. The goal is to build up heat from the friction to help burnish the hardeners in the oil and set the finish. If using a pure tung oil (without hardeners), the piece will need to sit for a long while to cure. After the oil has set, I like to use a friction polish with fine abrasives mixed in, such as Yorkshire Grit—multiple coats at a high RPM will really make the resin shine. The final step is to charge a buffing wheel with jeweler's polish and buff the piece to a glasslike finish. You'll get a feel for this process after a bit.

Sign the Piece

Last but not least, sign the bottom of your piece with a woodburner.

TROUBLESHOOTING

If you have followed the three golden rules of working with resin, you shouldn't have too many problems with your casting and turning. However, if an issue does arise, check out this list of troubleshooting advice.

 There are bubbles in the finished project. Bubbles can be broken down into two categories: process bubbles or moisture bubbles (see photo below).

Process bubbles happen in one of three ways. The first way is you did not get the mold in the pressure pot quickly enough and the resin started to set, not allowing the pressure to do its job. The second way is not using enough pressure on larger pours. The larger the volume of resin, the more pressure is needed to pulverize the bubbles. The third way is if no pressure pot was used at all.

Moisture bubbles are easy to identify because they almost look more like foaming that surrounds the wood and trails off the wood into the body of resin. This is an indicator that the wood, or whatever you are casting, was not properly dried, or water was introduced in some other way (such as through a water-based dye).

If the wood has been sitting on the shelf for a while, it's a good idea to **bake it** in the oven for 10 to 15 minutes before casting. This will ensure any surface moisture on the wood will be gone before it's time to cast.

It's also a good idea to place your **molds in the oven** before casting to evaporate any surface moisture, though you can only do this with UHMW molds or those secured with screws and not hot glue (or they'll start to break down in the heat).

The leftmost blank was cast without pressure and also the wood was not dried; this piece was not prepped at all. It is exhibiting process bubbles. The middle blank has moisture bubbles. The blank on the right is perfectly cast, with no bubbles.

The wood floated to the top of the resin surface during pressurizing.

The piece was not properly secured to the bottom of the mold (see photo below). For smaller molds, the wood can be secured with **hot glue**.

If you're using a reusable UHMW mold, I recommend putting a screw in the bottom because sometimes glue will not work with the plastic.

On larger pours, remember there is a lot of heat generated from the chemical reaction that will turn hot glue back into a liquid, allowing the object to release and float to the surface. For this reason, on large pours I use a screw in a waste portion of the blank. If there is no waste spot in your blank, mix up two-part epoxy and use it to secure your piece.

 The blank won't come out of the mold.
Urethane mold release spray, such as Stoner, must be used in reusable molds; if it is not, the blank will stick. Another cause of the blank sticking is if you **removed it from the**

pressure pot too soon and the resin is still warm. If the blank has time to fully cure, it will release better.

 Resin is still tacky or soft in some areas.

The resin has **not been properly mixed**. I recommend using a paint-mixing paddle and a power drill to ensure proper mixing in a very short time. One myth about working with resin is that mixing it too fast whips bubbles into the resin. This is not true; the pressure pot pulverizes all the bubbles. Even with using a paddle and a drill, you can have parts of the pour unmixed. It's very important to make sure you stop and scrape down the sides and I like to flip the drill into reverse to ensure all the resin is properly mixed.

 The mold leaked and most of the resin leaked out.

If there are gaps in your mold, this can happen. That is why I like to **seal the outer joints with hot glue** (see photo on p. 55). Hot glue is fast,

This burl was not properly secured in the mold and floated up.

easy, cheap, and will adhere to almost any surface. The best part is that it comes off easily; soak it with rubbing alcohol for a few minutes and it will break down and peel right off.

⚠ A void in the burl was revealed while turning.

If you want the void, you don't have to do anything. I have left voids in some of my pieces

Seal the outer joints of the mold to prevent resin leakage.

before. If you do not want the void, simply **fill it with resin**. Make a perimeter around the void with small pieces of wood (I like to use popsicle sticks). Cut them to fit and use hot glue to secure the frame. Fill the bottom of the pot with rice so you can level the piece to keep the resin from running out. The rest of the pressure process follows the guidelines on page 42.

⚠ Cracks occur on large pours.

This is a common issue in large pours. Though I do not have a 100% solution, I do have some tips to minimize occurrences.

Use MDF for the mold. As the resin shrinks while it cures, the MDF will move with it, helping to keep it from cracking.

Try to plan your pour to keep the **mass close to the same thickness** throughout the piece. As the resin begins to cure, it will set up in different areas at different times depending on the thickness. The goal is to try to keep the resin at the same thickness so everything is setting at the same time.

If you use an MDF mold, an even-thickness pour, a long cure time, and slow pressure release, you've done all you can to avoid cracks in large pours like these.

The chipping and shattering seen here is due to a dull tool, a slow lathe speed, or a fast tool travel speed.

Leave the mold in your pressure pot until the **core has cooled down**. It is not uncommon for me to leave large pours under full pressure (80 psi) for over 24 hours.

The final tip is to **slowly evacuate the compressed air** out of the pressure pot. No need to get in a hurry now... This is why I slowly release the air out of my compressor, allowing the atmosphere to slowly come back to normal.

Cracks are honestly not the end of the world. You have a few options to fix them so you do not ruin the whole piece. Small cracks can be filled with superglue. If the crack is larger, wait 24 hours, mix up a small batch of resin that matches the color, and recast, following the steps listed above to correct a hidden void.

⚠ **What was supposed to be a multi-colored piece ended up a muddy blend of colors.**
This is a common problem of using all liquid dyes. **Liquid dyes will blend together.** For example, if you pour blue and yellow with some red, where the colors meet you will get brown. If you use mica powder and allow the colors to intertwine on their own, the colors will stay separate and you will get a very cool effect.

Another cause is **moving the colors around** by hand too much. If you want to achieve a twirling pattern, use slow, flowing motions. Pretend you're writing in cursive. That is about the speed you want; any faster and you have a chance of mixing the colors, even when using mica powders.

⚠ **The resin shatters when it is turned.**
The most common cause of chipping or shattering resin (see photo at left) is a **dull tool**.

The second common reason is that your **speeds are not correct**. Either increase your lathe's RPMs, or slow down the feed rate of your tool.

⚠ **There are lines in the resin that aren't coming out.**
More than likely, you jumped **too high in grit level** when sanding and the grit paper you are currently using is not coarse enough to remove the more aggressive line. To find out what grit paper you need to go back to, rub the surface in the opposite direction with a sample of each grit less than what you are currently using. Once you see the line go away, you know where to start. Unfortunately, you will need to sand out the whole surface with this grit, ensuring you do not leave any transition lines.

The pressure pot will not hold pressure.
Your pressure pot has a **slow leak** somewhere. To find it, spray down all the fittings with soapy water. Where you see bubbles, tighten up the fitting until the leak stops. If you're casting, repair after you remove the blanks by applying plumber's tape to the threads. If none of the fittings are leaking, spray the soapy water between the top and the base. If you see bubbles, tighten up the clamp with a wrench. Over time the gasket will get worn and may need to be replaced if the leak will not stop.

 The vacuum pump cannot achieve the level of vacuum needed.
There may be a **leak in the fittings**. Cover the fittings with shaving cream. If there is a leak, you will see the shaving cream get drawn in. Repair the leak as needed; it might be as simple as applying a hose clamp over the fitting. The vacuum **pump may be too small** for the chamber, or the wrong pump for stabilizing. I recommend buying a chamber and pump from the same supplier. This way you know you are buying the correct pump for the job.

The vacuum pump is turned on but there is no vacuum at all.
The vacuum release **valve may be open**. If so, it will pull outside air through the system instead of the air from the chamber. The **lid may not be properly seated**. Try pushing the lid down with your hand and moving it around slightly. You should see the vacuum gauge begin to pull and bubbles begin to come out of the wood.

A hot water bath will make your urethane pourable again.

 The resin has been on the shelf for a while and the B part is very thick.
Over time, the B part will get very thick. There is no reason to be alarmed or throw the resin away. Simply fill the sink with the hottest water that comes out of your tap. **Place the bottle in the water** so the resin is equal to or below the resin line. Leave the bottle in the water until the water comes back to room temperature. Once the resin cools completely, you will notice that it has thinned out and is ready to use (see photo above).

PROJECTS

- - - - -

You understand the process; now let's make projects. Gather the General, Resin, and Turning Tool Kits (p. 139). You'll need these for each piece. Remember, you can create any of these projects with 100% resin blanks or wood that doesn't require stabilizing—go to your level of interest. We'll start off with a few approachable all-resin pieces so you can get the feel for resin on the lathe. First up in the lineup are some straight-forward **Kit Handles** to cut your teeth on (p. 60). Next up, a turning favorite—the **Pen** (p. 70). If you want to skip ahead to a resin-fusion blank, the first is the intriguing **Decorative Art** (p. 76). The next step is the **Bowl** (p. 84), when you'll bring your bowl-turning skills into play. Experience fusion faceplate-turning with the stunning **River Platter** (p. 92). The **Pine Cone Box** (p. 104) is a playful, yet elegant piece that will show you just how effective stabilizing resin can be. Finally, the most complex project is the **Hollow Form** (p. 117): create thin walls that show off the translucent quality of resin.

KIT HANDLES

■ ■ ■ ■ ■

Turning kits are a fantastic way to get the feel for turning with resin. With minimal tools and experience, you can make a practical and good-looking custom piece quickly. There are many kits available that include the necessary hardware to insert into a turned handle: beer taps, vegetable peelers, bottle openers, and so on. You can create four at a time by making a slab blank. We'll cover the general process for handles; also included are turning patterns and tips for wine stopper, ice cream scoop, and pizza cutter handles. **NOTE:** Never place a kit handle in the dishwasher; wash by hand.

TOOLS & MATERIALS

- Kit of choice
- Urethane resin, such as Alumilite Clear Slow, 1,060 g
- Red liquid urethane resin dye, such as Alumilite, enough to dye about 80% of the resin
- Gold mica powder, such as Pearl Ex, enough to dye about 10% of the resin
- Red liquid urethane resin dye and gold mica powder, enough to dye about 10% of the resin
- Urethane mold release spray, such as Stoner
- Mandrel and tap
- Four-jaw chuck and 60° live center
- 5-minute epoxy

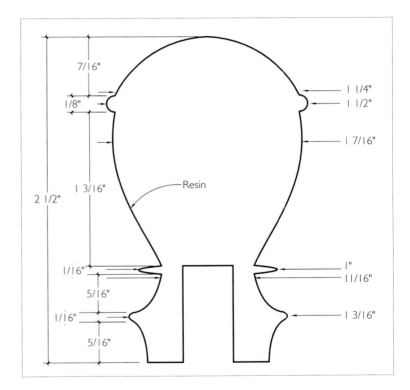

UHMW MOLD:

- Bottom (1): ¾" x 6 ½" x 6 ¼"
- Sides (2): ¾" x 6 ¼" x 3"
- End caps (2): ¾" x 7 ¾" x 3"
- Self-tapping flathead screws (32)

WINE STOPPER
The diameter of the base and the size of the hole are specific to the kit you use.

This project uses a ⅜" mandrel.

Step 2: The pictured stopper was tapped with a ⅜" tap.

Step 8: When done, take away the tailstock and shape the butt of the piece.

ICE CREAM SCOOP HANDLE

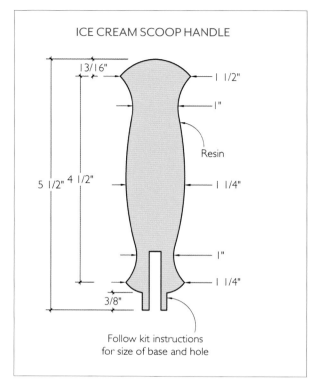

13/16"
1 1/2"
1"
Resin
5 1/2" 4 1/2"
1 1/4"
1"
1 1/4"
3/8"

Follow kit instructions
for size of base and hole

PIZZA CUTTER HANDLE

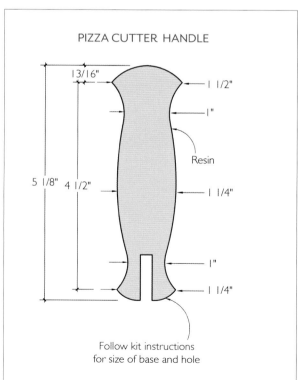

13/16"
1 1/2"
1"
Resin
5 1/8" 4 1/2"
1 1/4"
1"
1 1/4"

Follow kit instructions
for size of base and hole

ICE CREAM SCOOP

Since scooping ice cream requires a lot of side pressure on the handle, a longer threaded rod (and therefore drilled hole) is required. There is also a stainless-steel sleeve that slides over the blank for added strength. This project uses a ⅜" mandrel.

Before beginning the steps, be sure to make a ¼"-thick spacer with a ⅜" centered hole that is the same diameter as the inside dimension of the bushing from the kit.

Step 1: The pictured kit has a ⁵⁄₁₆"-diameter hole, ¼" longer than the threaded rod.

Step 2: As pictured, the handle was tapped with a ⅜" tap.

Step 5: First, measure the length of the tenon required to fit inside the assembled bushing and mark this on the blank. Then, mark ¾" back from there.

Step 8: Additionally, remove the material at the end of the handle until the tenon is flush with the spacer ring. Don't turn the head too small.

PIZZA CUTTER

This project is mounted with a four-jaw chuck and live center.

Step 1: My kit used a 12 or 12.5mm drill bit.

Make the Slab Blank

1. Cut out the mold. Cut the mold pieces from ¾"-thick UHMW.

2. Attach the mold pieces together. Attach the sides to the bottom with five or six panhead screws. The end caps are then attached with three screws in a vertical line on both ends, and five screws along the bottom of each side.

3. Add mold release spray.

4. Measure the resin. A 1½"-high pour yields three kit tool handles or six wine stoppers. Measure out how much you need of both parts. When you're ready to combine them, remember to start your stopwatch the second the two parts come together. The filled mold must be under pressure when the resin's open time runs out. Use the mixing attachment to combine evenly.

5. Add color. 80% of the resin is mixed with just red dye. 10% is just gold mica powder. 10% has both red dye and gold mica powder.

6. Pour. Add red resin first. Slowly pour both remaining mixes at the same time. Swirl with a toothpick.

7. Get it under pressure. Place the filled mold into the pressure pot. Close the lid securely and slowly begin adding air until you reach the correct psi for your resin. NOTE: Never exceed your pot's recommended pressure.

A side of the mold.

An end cap of the mold.

If you don't want to pour a slab blank, here are the dimensions for a single handle reusable mold:
- Bottom (1): ¾" x 1 ½" x 6 ½"
- Sides (2): ¾" x 6 ½" x 3"
- End caps (2): ¾" x 4 ½" x 3"
- This mold requires 331 g of resin.

Cut the slab blank into handle blanks.

8. Let the resin cure. Start a timer for the appropriate demold time for your specific resin, or let the setup sit overnight.

9. Slowly release the pressure from the pot. Remove the lid and take out the mold. Allow the mold to sit for 24 hours to ensure it is solid.

10. Separate the blank. Invert the mold over a solid surface to remove the slab blank. A few taps should release the blank.

11. Cut the slab into the pieces you need. Most handles are 1½" x 1½" x 6", while wine stoppers are usually 1½" x 1½" x 3".

Create the Handle

1. Drill the hardware hole. NOTE: The steps for making a kit handle are generally similar, but be sure to pay attention to the instructions that come with your particular kit. The hardware hole will need to be drilled to different depths and at different diameters. To start off, mark the center of the blank. Drill a hole into the blank as indicated by your kit instructions. You can use a drill press or the lathe.

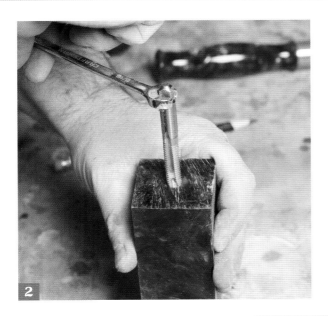

2. If your kit calls for a tapped hole, do it now. Remember to keep the tap perfectly aligned during the whole process.

3A. Mounting method: Mandrel. For kits with tapped holes, install a Jacobs chuck into the headstock and tighten the appropriately sized threaded mandrel into the chuck. Spin the blank onto the mandrel and bring the tailstock up.

3B. Mounting method: No mandrel. For kits without a mandrel, install the four-jaw chuck and your 60° live center into the tailstock. Install the blank into the lathe by bringing the tailstock forward and extending the live center into the hole that was drilled. The live center should fit right into the hole; if not, open the chuck and adjust the blank as needed.

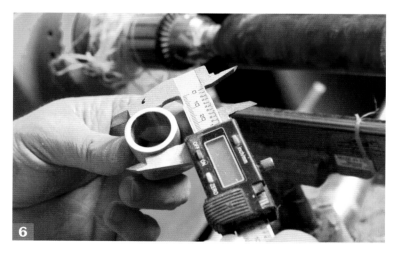

4. Round the blank. Make sure it doesn't become skinnier than what the hardware requires. Use your choice of carbide-tip tool, bowl gouge, spindle-roughing gouge, and parting tool at about 2,000 RPMs. Turn off the lathe.

5. Mark important spots. For most handles (not the wine stopper), mark a line approximately ¾" back from the end you drilled the hole in. This spot will act as a stop for your hand. Place your hand on the blank at the mark. Add another mark where your hand ends. This will help you shape the handle so it is comfortable to hold.

6. Measure the hardware. Take note of the diameter of the receiving end of the kit hardware. Depending on the kit, this is usually just cosmetic to ensure a nice transition from handle to hardware.

7. Shape the handle. At about 2,000 RPMs, shape the blank with a ½" bowl gouge and ⅜" spindle gouge, referring to the illustrations on pages 61 and 62. Cut in a design, stopping the lathe often to ensure a comfortable fit. Use a toothbrush to remove resin ribbons.

8. Size the end. Turn down the diameter on the tip of the blank at the tailstock end to match the diameter of the measurement that was taken in Step 6.

9. Dry-sand. Use dry sandpaper from 80 to 1,000 grit to smooth the surface (see process on p. 48).

10. Water-sand. Using Micro-Mesh pads, water-sand the handle from 2,400 up to 20,000 grit (see process on p. 49). Wipe the piece with water as needed.

11. Shine it up. Polish with a soft cloth and plastic polish of choice (see process on p. 50). Complete the process with the buffing wheel and jeweler's polish.

12A. Remove the piece: Mandrel. For kits with a mandrel, remove the handle from the lathe.

12B. Remove the piece: No mandrel. For kits without a mandrel, now is the time to cut away the blank from the chuck. Sand and shape the end of the handle by hand.

13. Install the hardware. Check the kit's instructions. Usually installation means applying a small amount of 5-minute epoxy into the hole, then screwing in the threaded insert.

14. Add the hardware. After the epoxy is dry, screw on the hardware. You're ready to use your new tool.

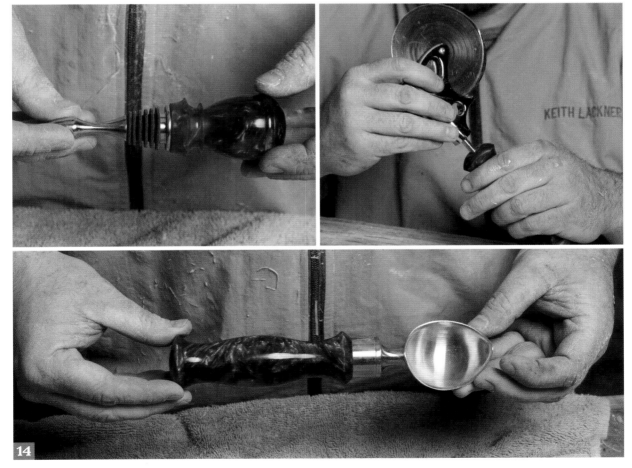

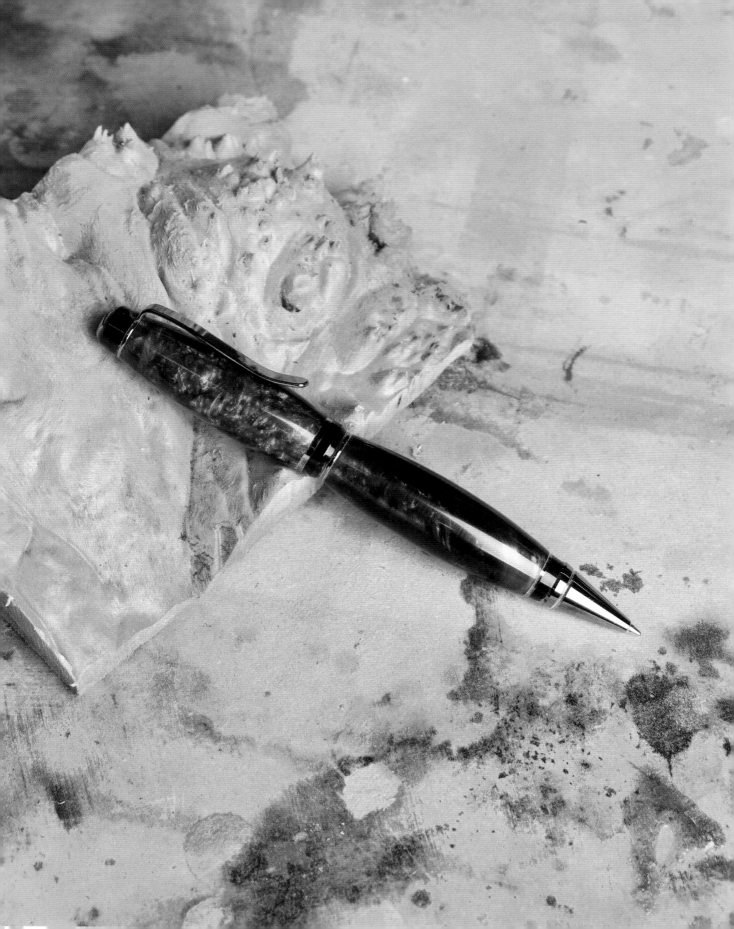

PEN

■ ■ ■ ■ ■

You're likely already familiar with the process of turning pens, so you can focus on the new material. Note that different kits require different blank sizes, drill bits, and bushing kits. Make sure to use the bushing sets made specifically for your kit. Here, I use a Premium Cigar Pen Kit with a 1" x 1" x 6" blank. Review the slab blank instructions on page 63 if you want to make a few of these; a 1"-high pour will yield six pen blanks. Otherwise, make a mold as described below that will yield a 1" x 1" x 6" blank.

TOOLS & MATERIALS

- Cigar pen kit
- Urethane resin, such as Alumilite Clear Slow, about 132 g
- Blue liquid resin dye, such as Alumilite, enough to dye about 30% of the resin
- Blue mica powder, such as Pearl Ex, enough to dye about 60% of the resin

- Pink mica powder, such as Pearl Ex, enough to dye about 10% of the resin Drill bit (kit specific)
- Reamer (kit specific)

- Mandrel (kit specific)
- Pen press or quick clamp
- Cyanoacrylate medium-density glue
- Accelerator

UHWM MOLD:

- Bottom (1): ¾" x 1" x 6"
- Sides (2): ¾" x 6" x 2 ½"
- End caps (2): ¾" x 2 ½" x 2 ½"
- Self-tapping flathead screws (22)

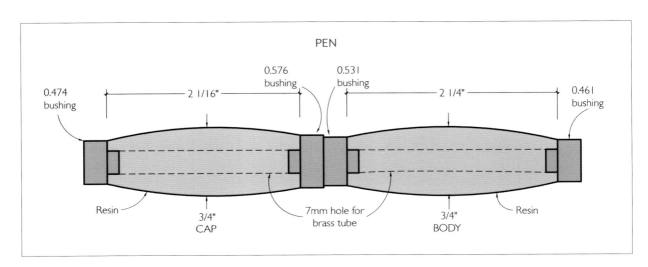

PEN

0.474 bushing — 2 1/16" — 0.576 bushing — 0.531 bushing — 2 1/4" — 0.461 bushing

Resin — 3/4" CAP — 7mm hole for brass tube — 3/4" BODY — Resin

1. Make the blank. Make the single-pen mold. Create a pen blank as shown on pages 40–43. Add the blue mica mixture first, then the blue-dyed mixure. Mix slowly with a toothpick. Drizzle in the pink mica mixture. Cast the blank. After curing, drill a hole through the center of both parts of the blank (size is specified in your kit).

> You can also make pen blanks with the slab mold from page 63; cast a 1" pour and cut the resulting slab into six blanks.

2. Prep the inserts. Use 100-grit sandpaper to rough up the smooth brass inserts. This step is important to ensure the cyanoacrylate will grab onto the inserts. See the difference between the sanded brass piece on the left and the smooth one on the right?

3. Glue the inserts. Apply cyanoacrylate to the brass inserts and a little in the holes of the blanks. Push the brass into the blanks so the brass pieces are sitting roughly $\frac{1}{32}$" below the surface on both sides. Spray with accelerator to set the cyanoacrylate.

4. Ream the blanks. Insert the reamer and flush up the blanks to the brass inserts. This process cleans the inside of the brass to remove any glue so the pen kit fits perfectly. It also levels the ends to 90° so there are no gaps when the kit is assembled.

5. Install the mandrel. Insert the mandrel into the lathe.

6. Place the bushings into the blanks. Consult the instructions for your kit. Secure the blanks onto the mandrel.

7. Round the blank. Use a bowl gouge or carbide-tipped tool. Remove the ribbons with a toothbrush every so often.

8. Shape the blanks. Create the desired profiles with a bowl gouge or carbide-tipped tool. Pay very close attention to ensure the edge of the blanks are flush with the bushings.

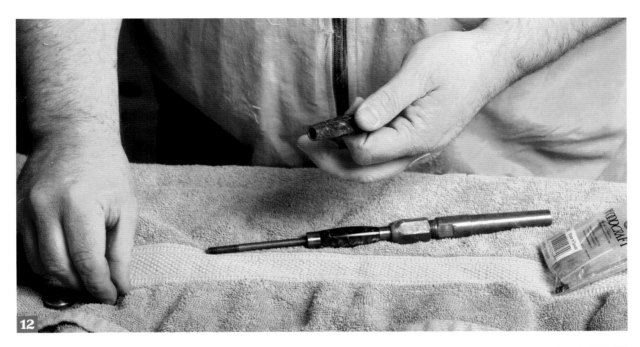

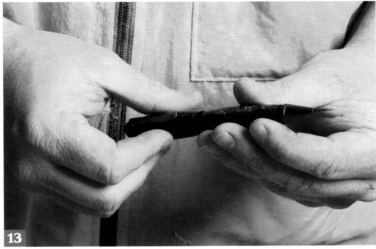

9. Dry-sand. Progress from 80 up to 1,000 grit (see process on p. 48).

10. Water-sand. With Micro-Mesh pads, work from 2,400 to 20,000 grit (see process on p. 49).

11. Apply polish. Buff at a high speed—3,000 RPMs or so (see process on p. 50).

12. Remove the parts from the lathe.

13. Assemble. Follow the kit instructions.

DECORATIVE ART

■ ■ ■ ■ ■

In the '90s, I found Jackson Pollock's work. I loved the movement throughout the paintings; everywhere you looked, there were colors blending and flowing together. Today, that style is called a "dirty pour." When I discovered resin casting, I wanted to try merging the techniques. With this type of piece, it's all about the natural flowing pattern of the resin as it freezes in time. The resin itself creates the art—I just help it come out for everybody to see. This project is all about showcasing the resin.

TOOLS & MATERIALS

- Burl, 6" x 6" x 3" (or what you can find)
- Urethane resin, such as Alumilite Clear Slow, about 2,000 g
- Gold mica powder, such as Pearl Ex, enough to dye about 3% of the resin
- Orange liquid resin dye, such as Alumilite, enough to dye about 3% of the resin
- Waste blank for jam chuck

MDF MOLD:

- Interior dimensions: 6" x 6" x 7" (or sized to fit the burl you have)

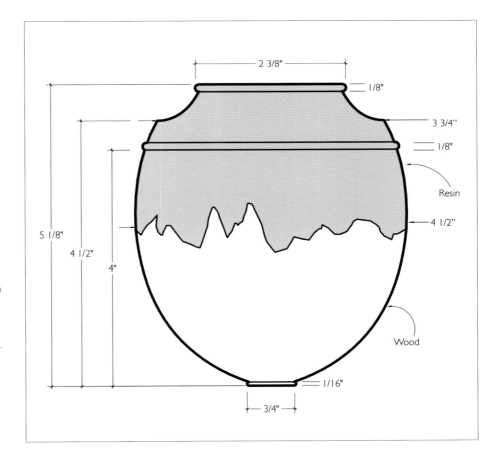

1. Cast your blank. First, find a burl, cut it to fit, and attach it to the bottom of the mold. Fill the mold about 94% with clear resin. Mix about 3% of the resin with gold mica powder and drop it in over the clear. Mix the last 3% of the resin with orange dye. Hold it high above the mold and carefully pour a stream. The orange resin will hit the mold at a higher speed, creating a cool splash pattern. Both colors will slowly drop into the clear resin until they are suspended in motion as the resin cures. This effect yields the best results and patterns in a solid mass of resin. See notes about the casting process on pages 40–43.

2. Round it. Cut off the corners of the blank on the bandsaw.

3. Get ready to turn. Mount the blank between centers.

4. Cut a tenon. Round the blank and cut in a tenon to mount it into your four-jaw chuck. Mount the blank into the chuck.

5. Transfer marks. Using the illustration as a reference, add marks to the blank so you know how to shape the curves into a vase profile that is pleasing to the eye.

6. Shape the blank. I like shapes that start out small and flow up, then come back slow. I think a gradual curve is more pleasing than a lot of movement. In this case, I'm showing off the beauty of the resin, so the last thing I want is a busy shape as a distraction. Don't forget to shape the top of the piece.

7. Sand the blank. (See intermediate process on p. 50.) Since this blank really needs to have the resin pop, it is important to really take your time and not jump grits. Apply Yorkshire Grit to the resin and turn the lathe up to roughly 2,500 RPMs. Apply multiple coats to ensure a clear finish. Remove the project blank from the lathe.

8. Shape the jam chuck. Place the waste block in the lathe and round it at 1,500 to 2,000 RPMs.

9. Measure for the jam chuck opening. Measure the widest part of the project.

10. Mark the opening. Transfer the measurements to the jam chuck blank.

11. Create the opening. Remove the material until you get a jam fit.

12. Insert the piece. Place the blank into the opening and secure it with the tailstock. Use a paper towel to prevent scuffing; trim it close to the piece.

13. **Turn away and shape the bottom.** Set RPMs at about 600. With a bowl gouge, complete the curve, removing the bottom. Turn a very small foot—approximately ¾" in diameter and no taller than ¹⁄₁₆"—the shorter the better. This will create a shadow line, giving your piece a lift as if it's hovering.

14. **Finish this end.** Dry-sand from 80 to 1,000 grit. Apply a penetrating oil to the wood with the piece still in the lathe (see intermediate process on p. 50).

15. Smooth the bottom. Remove the piece from the lathe. Cut off the nub left behind from the tailstock and sand by hand.

16. Polish it up. Apply Yorkshire Grit to the resin portion of the piece. Install the buffing wheel in the lathe, add jeweler's polish, and buff the piece to a high shine.

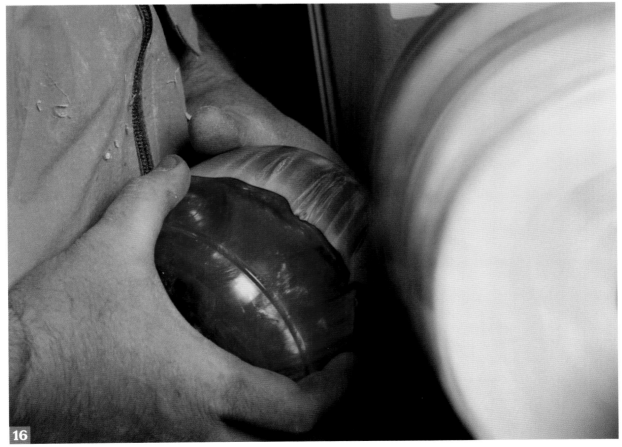

BOWL

■ ■ ■ ■ ■

Fusing a funky burl with some swirly, colorful resin makes for a great bowl. The combination of translucent and opaque materials creates a piece that really draws the eye. The impervious nature of urethane resin and a durable finish allows you to actually use this bowl if desired—or place it in a spot where it can be admired as a piece of art.

TOOLS & MATERIALS

- Burl, 6" x 6" x 2" (or what you can find)
- Urethane resin, such as Alumilite Clear Slow, about 1,200 g
- Green liquid resin dye, such as Alumilite, enough to dye about 90% of the resin
- Orange liquid resin dye, such as Alumilite, enough to dye about 5% of the resin
- Gold mica powder, such as Pearl Ex, enough to dye about 5% of the resin
- Hot glue
- Waste block, 3" dia. x 4"
- Polyurethane wipe-on finish, such as Arm-R-Seal

MDF MOLD:

- Interior dimensions:
  6" x 6" x 4"
  (or sized to fit the burl you have)

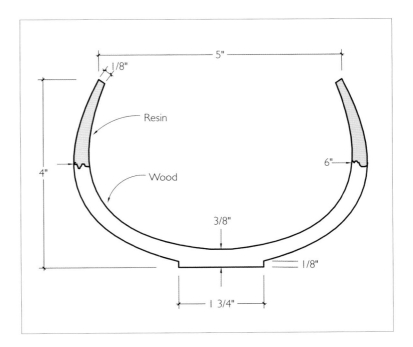

1. Cast your blank. (See pp. 31–43.) Cut a burl to fit and attach it to the mold bottom. Pour the green-dyed resin in first. Add layers of mica powder mixture (order doesn't matter) over the top to create a ribbon of colors. Complete the casting.

2. Prepare to mount. Round the blank on the bandsaw and mark the center on both sides. Install the drive and live center into the head and tailstock. Attach a waste block to the bowl base (wood end of this blank) with hot glue so there isn't any material lost from the blank when shaping the tenon. The waste also allows easy shaping of the base.

3. Mount the blank. Place the blank between centers and tighten the tailstock. Apply hot glue around the junction of the waste wood and the blank.

4. Turn the lathe on. Slowly bring the lathe up to speed for rounding the blank—start at 1,000 RPMs and gradually increase after the blank becomes rounded.

5. Center the blank. Once the blank has been rounded, cut in the tenon for the chuck with a parting tool. Remove the drive center and install the four-jaw chuck. Secure the blank into the chuck. The blank will be a little out of balance. Take a slight pass across the blank to ensure everything is centered. A bowl gouge or carbide-tip tool is best for this.

NOTE: For proper tenon size, see page 27.

6. Shape the outside. With a bowl gouge, shape the outside using either a push or a pull cut. Leave material directly in front of the chucks to ensure the cutting tool will not contact with the steel jaws of the chuck.

7. Dry-sand the outside to 600 grit. See process on page 48.

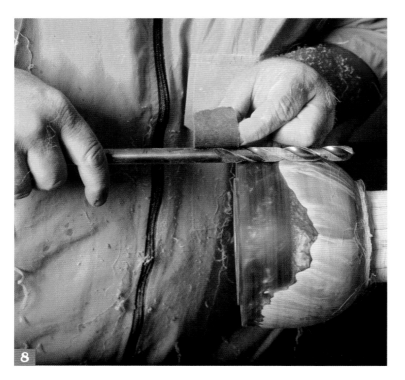

8. Drill the center. Measure the distance from the rim to the base, leaving ½" wall thickness on the bottom to allow for reverse turning. Transfer that distance to your drill. With the drill in the Jacobs chuck, drill down the desired depth.

9. Start creating the bowl. Using the carbide-tipped tool, start removing the resin from the bowl, starting just outside the hole you drilled. Work your way to the center in a slight arching motion. Continue these small cuts, ensuring a nice ribbon is coming off the end of your tool.

10. Even out the walls. Once you have reached the bottom of the drilled hole, now is the time to ensure an even wall thickness down the sides. At this point, the walls on the bowl should be approximately ¼" to ⁵⁄₁₆", gradually getting thicker toward the base.

11. Match the curve. Make sure there is a nice soft curve on the inside that matches the shape of the outside.

12. Sand the inside and mount.

Dry-sand the inside of the bowl to 600 grit (see process on p. 48). Remove the bowl from the jaws. Install cole jaws onto the chuck. If you do not have cole jaws, you can use a scrap block of wood to create a jam chuck, or use a vacuum chuck if you have one. When turning your bowl around, make sure you get it as close to center of the cole jaw as possible. Make sure to engage the live center of the tool stock into the piece to secure it in place.

13. Shape the bottom. Remove the extra material on the bottom of the bowl to match the curve of the bowl. It is very important at this stage to blend everything so the bowl has one flowing curve. A bowl gouge can take you the whole way through this process.

14. Shape the foot. Create a small step that is approximately one-third the width of the bowl. Clean up the bottom of the foot and blend the step into the foot. I prefer to either blend the curve into the foot or cut a very small foot into the step, giving the bowl some lift so it looks like it is floating. Always cut a slight bevel on the foot bottom so if your bowl does experience wood movement through the changing of the seasons, it will always sit true and flat without rocking.

15. Finish the bowl. Remove the tailstock; carefully remove the nub that was left from the live center being in the way. Dry-sand the bottom to 600 grit, blending all your curves and sand lines together (see process on p. 48). Since this is a bowl and will get used, I like to add a protective finish. First, apply a penetrating oil to the wood portion. On the entire piece, apply multiple coats of wipe-on polyurethane with a clean cotton rag, sanding with 0000 steel wool in between. I recommend three to five coats, but you could do more if you prefer.

14

15

RIVER PLATTER

■ ■ ■ ■ ■

The river platter is my version of a river table. I like to use figured natural-edged burls for this project, as I find the more visual movement you have, the better your piece will turn out. This is a display piece meant to be the center of attention on the table at special events or perched on your mantelpiece.

TOOLS & MATERIALS

- Large burl, roughly 3" x 4" x 12", cut with curves to fit in mold
- Urethane resin, such as Alumilite Clear Slow, about 3,000 g
- Blue liquid resin dye, such as Alumilite, enough to dye about 55% of the resin
- Blue mica powder, such as Pearl Ex, enough to dye about 30% of the resin
- Gold mica powder, such as Pearl Ex, enough to dye about 5% of the resin

- Green mica powder, such as Pearl Ex, enough to dye about 5% of the resin
- Purple mica powder, such as Pearl Ex, enough to dye about 5% of the resin
- Four-jaw chuck with worm screw

THROWAWAY MOLD:

- Sides (1): Concrete tube form, 12" dia. x 4"
- Bottom (1): MDF, 12" dia. x ½"

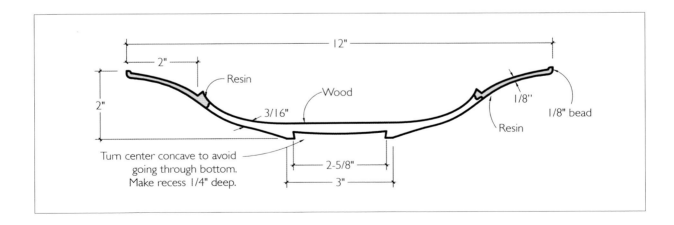

1. Create the mold. Follow the process on pages 35–36. Make your mold for this with a concrete tubing form from your local home center and an MDF bottom hot-glued in place. I recommend finding a few pieces of burl, cutting them to fit the curves, and attaching them to the bottom of the mold.

2. Add the resin. Pour in the blue resin first, then slowly add the blue, gold, green, and purple mica mixtures so they stay on top.

3. Make it flow. Gently use a thin stick to move the resin to resemble water rushing downstream. It's important not to mix the resin, but to use slow, flowing strokes. Allow 24 hours after casting for the resin to fully cure.

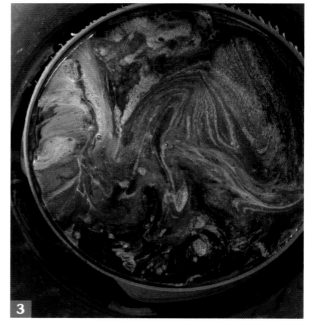

4. Prepare to mount. Mark the center on the face. Drill a hole to fit the worm screw, or drill on your face plate.

5. Get the lathe ready. Ensure the worm screw is mounted properly in the headstock.

6. Measure the outside of the chuck jaws. Lock down the jaws and use a set of veneer calipers to take the measurement. You will need to know this dimension later to make sure the jaws of the chuck are almost fully closed. This will ensure a tighter fit at that point.

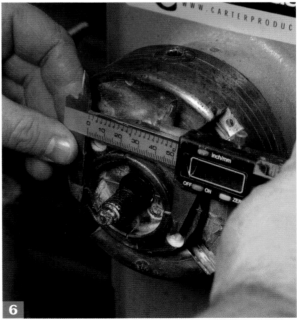

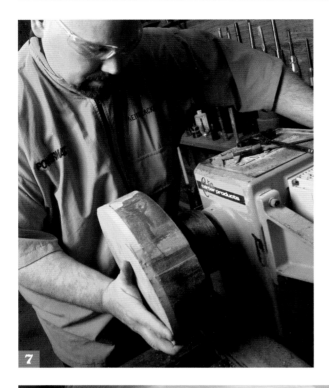

7. Mount up. Attach the workpiece to the lathe.

8. True up the blank. With the lathe at 1,000 RPMs, use either a bowl gouge or a carbide-tip tool to flatten the face of the blank.

9. Mark the chuck expansion. With the calipers, carefully mark the line for the chuck to expand into. This is done by touching only one side of the calipers to the wood and lining up the line to the opposite side of the calipers. Adjust as needed until the lines match up. NOTE: It is very important to only allow one side to make contact with the wood.

10. **Darken the line with a pencil.**

11. **Mark the foot.** Move over ⅜" and mark another line. These series of lines establish the foot.

12. **Mark up the design.** With the foot laid out, now it's time to lay out the design. I feel all platters deserve an elegant ogee profile. Measure from the edge of the foot to the edge of the platter. Mark a line in from the edge of the platter two-thirds of the total distance.

13. **Establish the rim.** I like to make my rims about ¼", so I mark ⁵⁄₁₆" for the rough-out stage.

14. **Start on the foot.** Cut in ¼" on the inside of the foot.

15. **Remove all material inside the foot.** Make sure to leave a cove on the bottom of this part to match the curve on the opposite side and reduce the risk of going through the bottom. Match the profile of the jaws and cut it into the side wall of the foot. If your jaws are dovetailed like mine, a recess will need to be cut to match the angle of the dovetails.

16. Shape the cove. Remove material, making a sweeping cove from the two-thirds line to the layout line for the rim.

17. Make the ogee. Shut the lathe off and measure once again from the line we drew for the foot to the rim. Split that in half and draw a line. Continuing with bowl gouge or carbide-tip tool, remove the material, making a gentle bead until the line we made at the halfway mark is gone. You should see a perfect ogee.

18. Establish the outside of the foot. Cut in $\frac{1}{16}$" to give your platter lift. It is very important not to cut in too far. When it comes time to reverse the platter and expand the jaws, you want to be sure you're locking onto solid wood or the jaws will break the foot.

19. Shape the foot. Cut a slight bevel on the bottom of the foot pointing inward. This will ensure the platter will always sit flat despite seasonal wood movement.

20. Prepare to sand. Use a bowl gouge to do a push cut or a shearing cut to prep the surface for sanding.

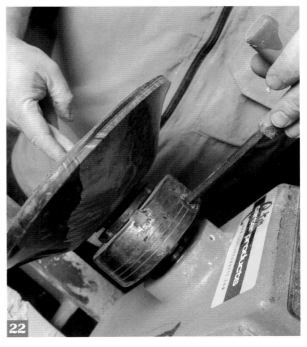

21. Sand and polish the surface.
See process on pages 48–52. I suggest dry-sanding to 1,000 grit, then applying penetrating oil to the wood, Yorkshire Grit to the resin, and finally buffing with jeweler's polish. Remove the piece from the lathe.

22. Mount the foot. Place the opening of the foot over the jaws of the chuck and open the jaws until they are locked. To ensure the blank is centered, push with your finger over the center hole while you open the jaws.

23. Position the tailstock. Slide the tailstock up to the workpiece and lock into position.

24. True up the face. With a series of scraping cuts, level the surface.

25. Cut away any excess material at the rim. Cut in the bead on the rim of the platter. Design the rim; I like to leave a 1½" to 2" rim, and at the base of the rim, cut in a small detail separating the two planes. This is purely cosmetic, but I think it is a nice feature.

26. Remove bulk of the wood.
Take off the tailstock. Make sure to
maintain an equal wall thickness
through the rim and get a little thicker
as you reach the bottom. Remember
the recess that was cut into the bottom
of the foot. The bottom needs to be a
little thicker to ensure you do not go
through it.

27. Finish the inside. Sand and
polish the interior of the platter as you
did the outside. Remove the project
from the lathe. Don't forget to sign
the bottom.

PINE CONE BOX

■ ■ ■ ■ ■

This piece received its inspiration from nature. My girlfriend and I love to take long walks with our dog. One of the paths we take near our home is called Pine Cone Path due to all the pine trees. A large Northern spruce tree supplied me with all the cones I needed. When I picked up the cones, I remember seeing the sky start to darken as the sun set, and I wanted to match the different blue tones I saw in the sky that night.

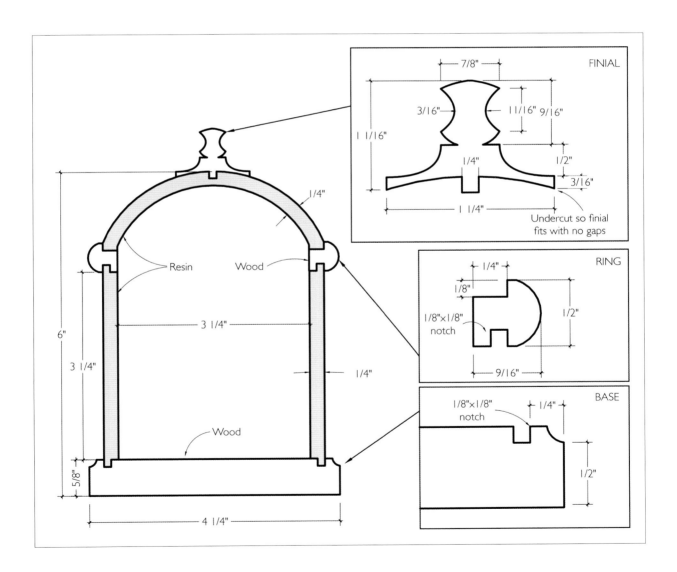

TOOLS & MATERIALS

- Pine cones (9)
- Urethane resin, such as Alumilite Clear Slow, 700 g
- Blue liquid resin dye, such as Alumilite, enough to dye about 65% of the resin
- White liquid resin dye, such as Alumilite, enough to dye about 10% of the resin
- Blue mica powder, such as Pearl Ex, enough to dye about 25% of the resin
- Wood blank for the bottom and top band, 2" x 5" x 5"
- Wood blank for finial, same species, 1 ½" x 1 ½" x 3"

- Four-jaw chuck with 5" jaws
- 5-minute epoxy
- Medium-density cyanoacrylate
- Accelerator
- Spray-on lacquer

PVC MOLD:

- Outside (1): 4" coupling pipe (4 ½" interior dia.) x 6"
- Inside (1): 2" pipe x 6"
- Lid (1): 4" coupling pipe (4 ½" interior dia.) x 3 ½"
- Bases (2): ¾" x 5" x 5" UHMW

1. Collect pine cones. Pick up cones that have fallen off the tree. This way, you know they are mostly dried out and have dropped most of their seeds. Bake them in the oven (p. 32) to draw out the remaining moisture. Stabilize them following the normal steps (pp. 32–33).

2. Make the mold. Start by using a small handheld rotary tool to grind away the stop inside the two 4" coupling PVC pieces (or mount on your lathe and turn it away). Mount UHMW to a waste block with hot glue. Measure the inner and outer dimensions of both the 4" and 2" PVC pipes with your calipers and transfer dimensions to the UHMW. Cut in a ¼"-deep groove to accept the PVC pipes. Secure the PVC pipes with hot melt glue and run another bead around the outside, just in case. Repeat steps for the lid; only one ring will be needed. You can watch a video of this process on my YouTube page.

3. Cast the blank. Follow the process on pages 31–43. Cut the seven base cones vertically to fit into the base; they will fit tightly. Place a strip of duct tape on top to make sure they don't pop out. The two cones in the lid are cut or broken up. Pour ½" blue resin into the base. Add one-quarter of white resin over the cones; allow it to flow all the way in. Add more blue, then drizzle blue mica resin (or add mica powder over the dye as it pours out). When ½" from the top, repeat adding white resin, saving one-quarter for the cap. Finish the base with blue mica and blue. For the lid, pour blue mica powder and blue resin together, stopping halfway up. Drizzle white over the pine cone ribs. Top with mica powder and blue. Add the remaining white in small ribbons. Cast the blank.

4. Mount the base blank. Position it in the chuck so the top of the blank is facing the tailstock.

5. Round the outside. With the roughing gouge, round the blank to approximately 4". If you find any voids in the pine cones as you turn, follow the steps on page 55 to fill them with resin. Cut in a tenon on the tailstock side to fit your four-jaw chuck.

6. Thin the walls. Remove the material inside the blank with a carbide-tip scraper until the wall thickness is roughly ¼". Don't reach in further than you feel comfortable with—we'll be flipping the piece around to access the other side shortly.

7. Dry-sand the inside. Start with 80 grit and work up to 1,000 grit (see process on p. 48). Remove the piece and rotate; put the piece back in the chuck with the tenon we just cut. True up the blank with a spindle-roughing gouge. Ensure an equal diameter down the whole outside of the blank. The finished diameter should be 3¾".

8. Fill in the gaps. This is where you may notice small gaps between the resin and pine cones. This is normal with pine cone castings. Apply small drops of medium-density cyanoacrylate glue to fill and spray with activator. Sand smooth with 150-grit paper. Dry-sand the outside to 1,000 grit (see process on p. 48). Remove the remaining thicker material inside the blank, ensuring an even ¼" wall thickness.

9. Cut a male tenon on both ends. This small tenon (about ⅛") is designed to accept the solid wood ring and base.

10. Remove the blank. Use a parting tool to separate the blank from the chuck just below the tenon.

11. Shape the wooden blank. Glue the solid wooden block for the base and top band to a waste piece of wood. Round and flatten the blank.

12. Transfer the tenon dimensions. Measure the tenon on the top of the pine cone base and transfer the measurements to the blank with the veneer calipers.

13. Cut the female tenon. Cut the matching tenon into the wood block so the resin blank fits snugly. Glue the blank onto the wooden piece with 5-minute epoxy. Use the lathe as a clamp. Once the glue dries, adjust the wall thickness of the bottom of the resin blank to ensure a perfect wall thickness all the way down the blank.

14. Make the top band. Measure the tenon as we did in Step 12. To create the top band, measure ½" down the wood blank and part off the blank.

15. Dry-sand the base. Clean up the freshly cut base and dry-sand to 1,000 grit (see process on p. 48). It is easier to do it at this point than when fully assembled. Cut in the tenon to accept the bottom of the pine cone blank and glue it into place.

16. Shape the wood. Once the glue is set, shape the wood portion and sand to 600 grit.

17. Flush the top ring. Cut away the inside of the top ring so the inside joint is flush.

18. Cut a dado for the lid to fit in.

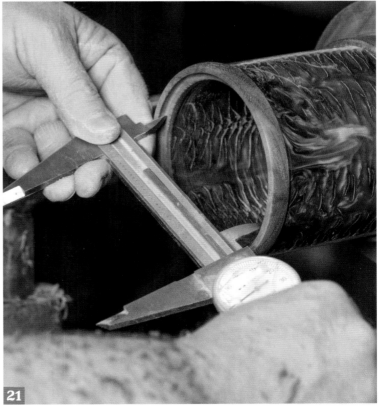

19. Mount the lid. Remove the blank and put your four-jaw chuck back on the lathe. Open the jaws and mount the resin lid blank.

20. Round the lid. Use a bowl gouge to round the lid edge.

21. Size the lid. Determine the size of the lid by measuring the opening the dado we cut into the band in Step 18 and transferring it to the blank with the calipers.

22. **Shape the inside of the lid.** Once the lid's dimension is established, draw out a template on a piece of paper and turn the inside to match the pattern. I like to use my round carbide-tipped tool to remove material. Compare by inserting the template until the inside matches. Dry-sand the inside of the lid to 1,000 grit.

23. **Test the fit.** Remove the lid from the lathe and place the lower resin section back on the lathe. Put the lid in place.

24. Tighten the fit if needed. If the fit is a little loose, a damp paper towel can be placed under the lid to ensure a snug fit. Trim the towel so it isn't much bigger than necessary.

25. Shape the outside of the lid. Bring in the tailstock and finish shaping the outside of the lid.

26. Make the finial hole. Once all shaping and sanding is done, remove the tailstock. Add blue tape to keep the lid in place and cut a ⅛" hole in the top of the lid to set the finial.

27. Begin shaping the foot. With a parting tool, remove base material until about ¼" diameter is left.

28. Remove the piece. With a handsaw, cut away the remaining material and separate the piece.

29. Prepare the waste wood. Measure the opening of the top of the base with calipers and transfer that dimension onto the waste block.

30. Shape the waste wood. Cut in a step up on the waste block to accept the box base. The goal is to achieve a snug fit.

31. Reverse-mount the base.
Place the base over the freshly cut step. Make sure the fit is tight and add blue tape to ensure the piece does not come off during this step.

32. Complete the foot. Turn
away the bottom of the foot. Sand to completion.

33. Shape the finial. Glue the
1½" finial blank onto the waste block. Turn and sand the finial to completion. I like to draw finials first and try to make them flow with the piece. I recommend using a ⅜" spindle gouge to access the tight transitions and blend the curves. Cut the ⅛" tenon to fit the hole in the lid.

34. Complete the box. To ensure a
good fit, undercut the underside of the finial. Remove and glue the finial to the lid with 5-minute epoxy. With this project, my finish of choice is a simple spray-on lacquer (see p. 50).

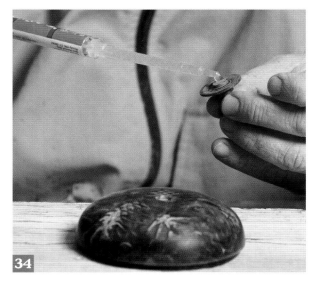

HOLLOW FORM

■ ■ ■ ■ ■

Reverence is a design I came up with after being influenced by world-renowned turner and craftsman Ray Key. Ray spent his life creating art and teaching students all over the world. I always thought I would have the opportunity to meet him and shake his hand, but sadly, he passed away before I ever got the chance. The day I learned of his passing I put my spin on one of his more famous shapes as a sign of respect to keep his spirit alive for the next generation of craftsmen.

TOOLS & MATERIALS

- Urethane resin, such as Alumilite Clear Slow, about 2,000 g
- Yellow liquid resin dye, such as Alumilite, enough to dye about 75% of the resin
- Gold mica powder, such as Pearl Ex, enough to dye about 5% of the resin
- Orange liquid resin dye and gold mica powder, enough to dye about 10% of the resin
- Orange liquid resin dye, such as Alumilite, enough to dye about 5% of the resin
- Red liquid resin dye, such as Alumilite, enough to dye about 5% of the resin
- Waste block for reverse-turning
- ¾" Forstner bit
- Drill bit extension (optional)
- Hollowing system, such as Carter Products Hollow Roller
- Hollowing gooseneck scraper
- Hemostat (I recommend a set with different curved ends)

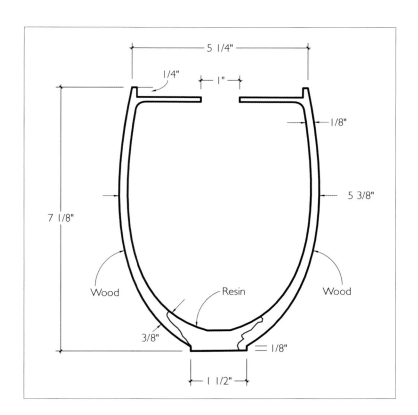

UHMW MOLD:

- Bottom (1): ½" x 5 ½" x 5 ½"
- Sides (2): ½" x 5 ½" x 7 ½"
- End caps (2): ½" x 7 ½" x 7 ½"

1. Cast the blank. Follow the process on pages 31–43. Choose a burl large enough to get both sections from the same cap. It's very important that the tones and the grain patterns match, especially the live edge sections. Do your best to place the burls so there is an about 2" opening running down the center, allowing the resin to be as centered as possible. With one hand, start slowly pouring the yellow-dyed resin. With your other hand, alternate pouring the other dyes so everything swirls together. Cast the blank.

2. Mount the blank. Find and mark center on both sides of the blank. Draw a circle on the end of the blank and cut it round on the bandsaw. Mount the blank between centers.

3. Round the piece. Slowly bring the lathe up to speed and round the blank.

4. Make a tenon. Establish a tenon to mount the piece into a four-jaw chuck.

5. **Remount the piece.** Put the tenon in the jaws. Even though we already rounded the piece, since we removed the piece from the lathe and remounted it, the work piece will be out of balance. Rebalance it. Shape the outside in a gradual curve down to the base.

6. **True up the face of the piece.**

7. Create a lip. Remove ¼" of the face, leaving a lip that is ¼" tall.

8. Prepare to hollow. Measure the length of the hollow form. Insert a Jacobs chuck into your tailstock. Insert a ¾" Forstner drill bit.

9. Mark the drill. Place tape on the drill ½" shorter than the length of the workpiece.

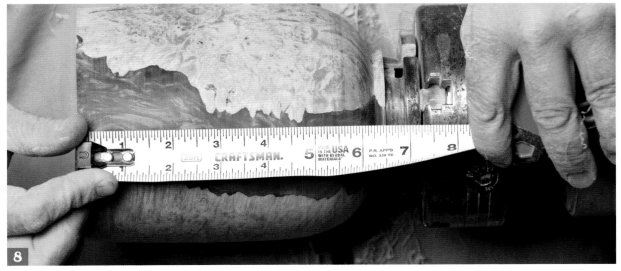

10. Start to bore. Turn on the lathe and begin boring out the center.

11. Keep it clean. Be sure to periodically clear out the chips.

12. Sand the outside. Now is the time to sand the face and the whole outside to completion. In this project, sanding is very important because the piece is transparent. Dry-sand from 80 to 1,000 grit. Water-sand to 20,000 grit. Apply Huts liquid plastic polish to the resin and use a clean cotton rag to burnish. Buff the outside with jewelry polish and buffing wheel.

13. Hollow it out. With your hollowing tool, remove the inside material (see drawing at right for the proper way to remove the inside material). Continue to remove material until a ⅛" wall thickness is left evenly throughout the piece, tapering to a ⅜"-thick bottom. The reason for this is to make the bottom heavier and more stable.

14. Sand the inside and finish up. Using a hemostat, wrap your sandpaper around a small piece of shop rag. Secure the paper in the clamp. Dry-sand from 80 to 1,000 grit. Water-sand to 20,000 grit. Polish the inside with Yorkshire Grit. Remove the piece from the lathe. Reverse-mount the piece with the waste block. Sand bottom to completion. Remove from the lathe and remove the small nub left behind from the tailstock. Finish sanding the foot by hand through the grits. Sign your piece with your name and date.

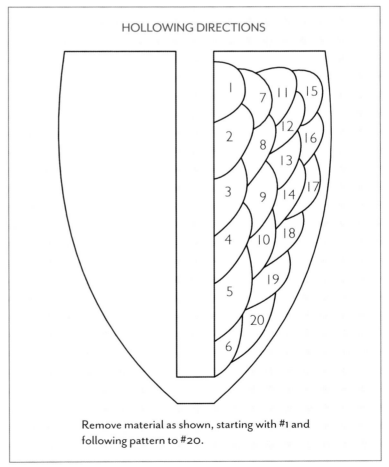

HOLLOWING DIRECTIONS

Remove material as shown, starting with #1 and following pattern to #20.

RESOURCES

■ ■ ■ ■ ■

You'll find plentiful inspiration and information in the following pages. A gallery of thought-stimulating finished resin projects will give you ideas to try out in your own shop, now that you understand how to work with urethane resin. If you need to find any of the special tools, materials, or equipment shown in the book, look no further than the manufacturer section. And don't miss the glossary if you want to brush up on resin-casting terms.

GALLERY

■ ■ ■ ■ ■

Hell Fire

As I mentioned earlier, when I first bought that pallet of walnut veneer blocks I had no idea what I was going to do with them, but I knew it would be something special. That first casting—*Hell Fire*—was the largest of its kind at the time, to my knowledge, and the largest turning I had attempted then. I remember thinking throughout the process how truly special this piece was going to be, and to this day, it is still one of my favorite pieces.

Over the years, my inventory of billets dwindled until I got down to my very last one. It was at that time I traveled once again to the David Marks school. During that class, David had a piece in process that I was able to see completed a few months later at a show we both attended in Atlanta, Georgia. This piece—*Sensei*—was the perfect example of what a master can create and symbolizes everything I strive to be.

When I got home, my mind kept going back to that piece. After months of drawing, I finally came up with a concept that was heavily influenced by it. I reached out to David and he gave me his blessing to create this piece. During the course of this build, I got stuck, especially on the frame, and would have to call my teacher to have him walk me through some of the steps. When I was finally done with this piece, I found that I pushed myself to another level of wood art that I didn't know I could do, and it wouldn't have been possible without the help of David and his original creation, Sensei. That is why I named this piece *Grasshopper*—through this whole build working under a master, I proudly called myself a young grasshopper to this sensei.

You can see the journey I took from the very first piece of walnut to the last, and how my skills evolved. *Hell Fire* pushed the envelope of casting on a single piece, using a full gallon of resin. *Grasshopper* used almost five gallons across two pieces of wood, attempted bent wood lamination, and incorporated a segmented top and a stand made from 256 segments of wood in just the ring alone. These two pieces show my path from the very beginning through the creation of my overall process, the development of the 3 Golden Rules, and pushing everything to the extreme. This is captured for the first time by these two pieces being brought back together for this book.

Grasshopper

Scorched Earth

Smoldering

Green Hazer

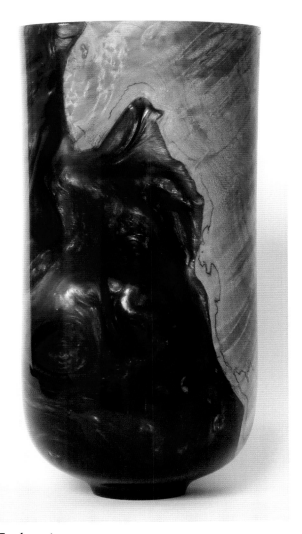

Exploration

Independence

Cosmos

Lilac Fusion

Mystic Winds

Sahara

Indian Trail

Anubis

Frosty

Vibrant Explosion

Latitudes

Purple Haze

Gaia

Forgotten Earth

Shattered Sea

Lightning Strike

RICE TO RESIN CONVERSION CHART FOR ALUMILITE CLEAR SLOW

Total Cups by Volume	Total Grams of Resin	Total Part A in Grams	Total Part B in Grams
1	265	133	133
2	530	265	265
3	795	398	398
5	1325	663	663
6	1590	795	795
7	1855	928	928
8	2120	1060	1060
9	2385	1193	1193
10	2650	1325	1325
11	2915	1458	1458
12	3180	1590	1590
13	3445	1723	1723
14	3710	1855	1855
15	3975	1988	1988
16	4240	2120	2120
17	4505	2253	2253
18	4770	2385	2385
19	5035	2518	2518
20	5300	2650	2650
21	5565	2783	2783
22	5830	2915	2915
23	6095	3048	3048
24	6360	3180	3180
25	6625	3313	3313
26	6890	3445	3445
27	7155	3578	3578
28	7420	3710	3710
29	7685	3843	3843
30	7950	3975	3975

RICE TO RESIN CONVERSION CHART
FOR MEASURED BY WEIGHT/VOLUME RATIO

If you use a resin other than Alumilite Clear Slow, you can fill in this chart to use as a quick reference. If the resin you use is measured by weight and mixed 1:1, weigh 1 cup of each Part; record the heaviest one in both columns in the 2 Total Cups line and do the math to fill in the rest of the cells. Otherwise, consult the manufacturer's website or the label on the resin to fill in the chart.

Total Cups by Volume	Total Resin	Total Part A	Total Part B
1			
2			
3			
5			
6			
7			
8			
9			
10			
11			
12			
13			
14			
15			
16			
17			
18			
19			
20			
21			
22			
23			
24			
25			

MANUFACTURERS

ALUMILITE:
Clear Slow urethane resin and dyes.
www.Alumilite.com

CALIFORNIA AIR:
Pressure pot.
www.CaliforniaAirTools.com

CARTER AND SON TOOLWORKS:
Traditional turning tools.
CarterAndSonToolworks.com

CARTER PRODUCTS:
Carbide-tip tools; bandsaw blades.
CarterProducts.com

GLOBAL WOOD SOURCE:
Burls.
www.GlobalWoodSource.com

GENERAL FINISHES:
Seal-A-Cell and Arm-R-Seal finishes.
GeneralFinishes.com

HUT PRODUCTS:
Plastic polishes.
www.HutProducts.com

JACQUARD PRODUCTS:
Pearl Ex mica powder.
www.JacquardProducts.com

**MICRO-SURFACE
FINISHING PRODUCTS, INC.:**
Micro-Mesh sanding products.
Micro-Surface.com

MIRKA, LTD.:
Abranet sanding products.
www.Mirka.com

POWERMATIC:
Lathes; dust collection; bandsaws.
www.Powermatic.com

STONER MOLDING SOLUTIONS:
Mold release sprays.
www.StonerMolding.com

THE BEALL TOOL COMPANY:
Buffing wheels; turning tools.
Bealltool.com

THOMPSON LATHE TOOLS:
Traditional turning tools.
ThompsonLatheTools.com

TMI PRODUCTS:
Stick Fast cyanoacrylate glues.
www.TMIProducts.net

TURNTEX, LLC:
Cactus Juice stabilizing resin and equipment.
www.TurnTex.com

YORKSHIRE GRIT:
Friction polish.
Yorkshire-Grit.com

TOOLS YOU'LL NEED

GENERAL TOOL KIT

- Ruler or tape measure
- Pen, pencil, or marker
- Cutting method of choice
- Drill with twist drill bits and screwdriver bits
- Sandpaper, such as Abranet, in 80, 120, 220, 320, 400, 600, and 800 grits
- 0000 steel wool
- Surface-cured finish of choice
- Penetrating finish of choice
- Woodburner

TURNING TOOL KIT

- Face shield, safety glasses, and mask
- Lathe
- Jacobs chuck
- Four-jaw chuck, Cole jaws, drive center, and live center
- Veneer calipers
- Elliptical bowl gouges: ⅜", ½"
- Spindle gouge: ⅜"
- Spindle-roughing gouge: ¾", 1", 1¼"
- Parting tool: ⅛"
- Backsaw
- Toothbrush
- Sharpening system of choice

RESIN TOOL KIT

- Rubber gloves, glasses, and mask
- Moisture meter
- Wirebrushes
- Wood chisel
- Dental picks
- Vacuum chamber
- Vacuum pump
- Stabilizing resin
- Oven with tray
- Rice
- Scale with gram measurements
- Clear plastic containers with volume marks
- Stopwatch
- Drill and mixing attachment
- Scraper
- Reusable molds
- Thin stick for colored resin manipulation
- Urethane mold release spray, such as Stoner
- Pressure pot
- Air compressor
- Replaceable carbide-tip round-nose tool, such as Keith Lackner signature tool
- Water-sanding pads, such as Micro-Mesh, in 2,400, 3,200, 4,000, 6,000, 8,000, 12,000, 15,000, and 20,000 grits
- Plastic polish, such as HUT Ultra Gloss Plastic Polish, and soft cloth
- Friction polish, such as Yorkshire Grit
- Jeweler's polish and buffing wheel

GLOSSARY

CASTING As a noun, refers to the in-process or hardened resin blank. As a verb, describes the process of creating such a blank.

CURE TIME The amount of time until the mixed resin is completely hardened.

DEMOLD TIME The amount of time that must pass before mixed resin is hardened enough to remove from a mold.

EPOXY RESIN A liquid two-part plastic that cures into an extremely rigid state. It has a long open time and requires heat to break up bubbles.

40/40 GRIND The recommended grind on an elliptical bowl gouge for turning resin. The angle of the cutting edge is 40° and the wings are swept back at 40° for better chip removal.

MICA POWDER A great way to color urethane resin and layer different shades without creating a muddy mess. Also adds sparkle to the resin.

MIX RATIO The proportions of the two resin parts that must be mixed together to properly harden. Resins can have a ratio by weight or by volume.

OPEN TIME The amount of time mixed resin will remain in liquid form and workable. Also called work time and pot life.

POLYESTER RESIN A liquid two-part plastic that cures into a hard and brittle state. Used with fiberglass in the automotive and marine industries, and not useful for turning and crafting projects.

POT LIFE See Open time.

PRESSURE POT Together with an air compressor, a pressure pot exerts air pressure on whatever is placed inside. For resin projects, this is used to compress bubbles in the still-liquid resin so they are too small to see when the resin hardens.

RELEASE SPRAY Used on reusable molds to prevent the blanks from sticking to the mold.

RESIN FUSION Pieces made from wood and resin.

REUSABLE MOLD A mold for creating a resin or resin-fusion blank that is made from PVC, UHMW, or silicone. These molds are meant for production pieces, or a type of blank that is created repeatedly. These molds can be purchased or made by hand. When coated with mold release spray, these molds are usually simple to remove castings from and can be used again immediately.

SLAB BLANK A resin blank that is not used as-is, but rather is cut apart into different pieces. For example, into several different handle blanks.

STABILIZING Saturating a soft piece of wood with stabilizing resin and then heating it to harden completely. Stabilized woods will not be dyed by colored resins, are easier to use in a resin-fusion piece, and will not experience seasonal wood movement. However, there are plenty of resin projects turners can make without having to stabilize anything.

STABILIZING RESIN A resin that is used to penetrate wood grain and becomes rigid when heated.

THROWAWAY MOLD A mold that is custom-made from MDF and other disposable materials for a unique or unusually shaped blank. It is cut away and disposed of when the casting is complete.

ULTRA-HIGH MOLECULAR WEIGHT PLASTIC A type of plastic that is durable and difficult for resin to stick to, so it is useful as a material to create reusable molds. Abbreviated as UHMW.

URETHANE RESIN A liquid two-part plastic that cures into a hard but semi-rigid state. This type of resin machines very well. It has a short open time and must be placed in a pressure pot to eliminate bubbles. Avoid moisture. This type of resin is the focus of this book.

VACUUM CHAMBER In concert with a vacuum pump, a vacuum chamber removes all air from whatever is placed inside. For resin projects, this is used to stabilize wood.

WORK TIME See Open time.

INDEX

Note: Page numbers in *italics* indicate projects. Page numbers in **bold** indicate gallery pieces.

ABOUT THE AUTHOR

■ ■ ■ ■ ■

Keith's passion is creating and pushing the envelope on new one-of-a-kind pieces. His love for exotic woods helped him become one of the founding artists in the current resin trend. As the foremost artist and instructor in woodturning with resin, he has taught people from all over the world the steps he has honed over the years. His expertise not only in casting but also in woodturning means he can teach students every step of the process, from casting to design to turning to finishing. Keith has showcased his wood and resin pieces in galleries all over the United States, and has numerous articles in *Woodcraft Magazine* and *Woodturning.* He is a sponsored woodturner for Carter Products and Powermatic, and has instructed at the Marc Adams School of Woodworking, as well as many other venues and conferences across the country.

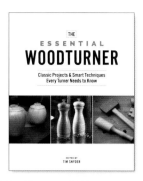
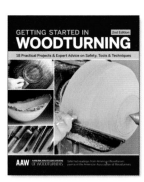

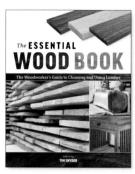

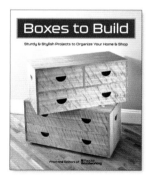